DA CAPO PRESS SERIES IN
ARCHITECTURE AND DECORATIVE ART
General Editor: ADOLF K. PLACZEK
Avery Librarian, Columbia University

Volume 9

A SILVER COLLECTORS' GLOSSARY

and

A LIST OF
EARLY AMERICAN SILVERSMITHS
AND THEIR MARKS

A SILVER COLLECTORS' GLOSSARY

and
A LIST OF
EARLY AMERICAN SILVERSMITHS
AND THEIR MARKS

HOLLIS FRENCH

DA CAPO PRESS • NEW YORK • 1967

A Da Capo Press Reprint Edition

An unabridged republication of the
first edition published in New York
in 1917 by The Walpole Society in
an edition of two hundred copies.

Library of Congress Catalog Card Number 67-27454

Da Capo Press
A Division of Plenum Publishing Corporation
227 West 17 Street, New York, N. Y. 10011

Printed in the United States of America

A LIST OF
EARLY AMERICAN SILVERSMITHS
AND THEIR MARKS

WITH A
SILVER COLLECTORS' GLOSSARY

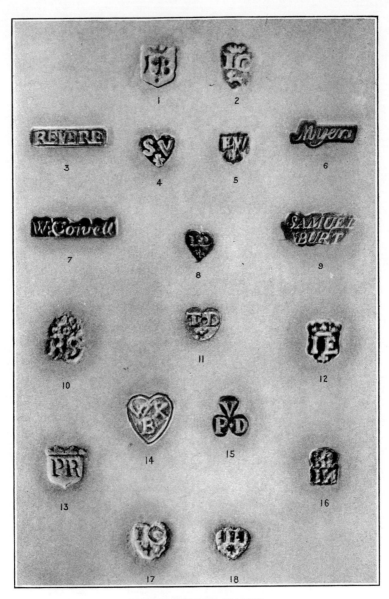

SILVERSMITHS' MARKS

1. *John Burt*	7. *William Cowell*	13. *Paul Revere, Sr.*
2. *John Coney*	8. *Jeremiah Dummer*	14. *Benjamin Wyncoope*
3. *Paul Revere*	9. *Samuel Burt*	15. *Peter Van Dyke*
4. *Samuel Vernon*	10. *Robert Sanderson*	16. *John Hull*
5. *Edward Winslow*	11. *Timothy Dwight*	17. *John Coney*
6. *Myer Myers*	12. *John Edwards*	18. *John Hull*

THE WALPOLE SOCIETY
A LIST OF
EARLY AMERICAN SILVERSMITHS
AND THEIR MARKS

BY

HOLLIS FRENCH

WITH A

SILVER COLLECTORS' GLOSSARY

NEW YORK
PRINTED FOR THE SOCIETY
MCMXVII

THE WALPOLE SOCIETY

LIST OF MEMBERS

Francis Hill Bigelow
Dwight Blaney
Thomas Benedict Clarke
George Francis Dow
Alexander Smith Cochran
Henry Wood Erving
Harry Harkness Flagler
Hollis French
R. T. Haines Halsey
Norman Morrison Isham
Henry Watson Kent
Luke Vincent Lockwood
Marsden J. Perry
Charles Munn
Albert Hastings Pitkin
Frederick Bayley Pratt
Charles Russell Richards
George Smith Palmer
Philip Leffingwell Spalding
Charles Hitchcock Tyler
George Parker Winship
Theodore Salisbury Woolsey
John Munro Woolsey

COMMITTEE ON SILVER

PREFACE

IN continuation of its policy of publishing from time to time information of value to collectors, the Walpole Society issues herewith this list of American Silversmiths and their marks with a Glossary, uniform with its previous publications on Furniture and Ceramics.

Nothing at present exists in this country on the subject which is comparable to the exhaustive works which have been published abroad on the English silversmiths and their art, and while it is realized that the time is perhaps not yet ripe for such books on their American confrères, it is believed that these data on American silversmiths, followed by the short glossary of terms used in describing silver, will be of benefit to those interested in collecting early American silver.

Most of the information concerning the early workers of silver in this country is scattered through various catalogues of exhibitions or sales, so that there is no place to which a collector can turn for concise data to identify a piece or to understand its description.

Although a considerable amount of work was required to collect the information published in this volume, no claim for originality is made, and acknowledgment is freely offered to those who have so laboriously searched the early records for many of the facts herein set forth.

The debt which every silver collector owes to R. T. H. Halsey it were almost superfluous to mention. Without the information which he has so patiently gleaned and freely published, especially in his introduction to the catalogue "American Silver," published by the Boston Museum of Fine Arts in 1906, and in his "Notes on Early New York Silversmiths," printed in the catalogue of an exhibition of silver at the Metropolitan Museum of Art in 1911, it would be difficult to know where to find data on most of the early makers. Special

acknowledgment is also made for the many names of silversmiths, and their dates and marks, which Francis H. Bigelow
has found in his researches and has so generously given me.

From those other members of our Society, the late George
M. Curtis, and his work "Early Silver of Connecticut and its
Makers," from Dr. Theodore S. Woolsey, the dean of Ameri-
can silver collectors, and from L. V. Lockwood, Dwight
Blaney, H. W. Kent and George S. Palmer much valuable
information has been obtained.

To Judge A. S. Clearwater, who so kindly offered the use
of his great collection for study, and to Miss Florence V. Paull
of the Museum of Fine Arts, Boston, many thanks are due,
and acknowledgment must also be made for data from E.
Alfred Jones' work on "American Church Silver," as well as
from J. H. Buck's "Old Plate."

The Museum of Fine Arts in Boston and the Metropolitan
Museum in New York have helped, so materially in the
compilation of facts for this catalogue, and both have so kindly
permitted the use of data from their publications, that it is a
pleasure to acknowledge here their assistance.

Very little attempt has been made to collect data on silversmiths working early in the nineteenth century. The growth
of the country at that time led to a great demand for silver
and consequently to an increase in the number of silver workers,
but the decadence of art then prevalent affected the product
of the silversmiths, as it did the work of craftsmen in the allied
arts. Collectors are, therefore, more interested in the earlier
makers, and consequently but little effort has been made to
catalogue silversmiths working after 1820.

It is a matter of regret that the original intention of publishing only enlarged photographic reproductions of the marks, a
few of which are illustrated in the frontispiece, had to be given
up for compelling reasons. There is probably nothing more ac-
curate or satisfactory than a good photograph for studying
marks, but unfortunately many of the latter are so worn that a
clear negative is impossible. Under these circumstances only
a drawing will properly represent the mark as it was originally.

PREFACE

It is believed, however, that the reproductions made from these drawings will prove satisfactory, but it should be remembered that, as a matter of clearness, the imprints are in all cases made about twice the size of the originals.

When no copy of a mark could be made, the description has been given by type in a suggestive manner, but there are still many makers of whom no marks have yet been discovered, and conversely many marks which cannot with accuracy be attributed to any known maker.

There is still, therefore, much work to be done on the subject, and it is realized that the present publication is only a beginning, which it is hoped others will carry on.

Rubbings or descriptions of marks other than those here published and the receipt of information concerning them will be gratefully received by the author who is well aware of the deficiencies of the work.

The glossary of silver terms following the data on silversmiths has been almost entirely prepared by Dr. Theodore S. Woolsey.

HOLLIS FRENCH

LIST OF
EARLY AMERICAN SILVERSMITHS
AND THEIR MARKS

The following abbreviations have been used in the text:

b	= born	e	= emigrated	
bap.	= baptized	f	= freeman	
c	= circa	m	= married	
d	= died	n.a.f	= not admitted freeman	
D	= directory	w	= working	
	(?)	= in doubt		

SILVERSMITHS AND THEIR MARKS

A

ABBOTT, J.   *Portsmouth, N. H.*
[*mark*]   Name in capitals in rectangle

ACKLEY, E.   c. 1800

    Small shaded Roman capitals in
                        rectangle

ADAMS, J.   *Alexandria, Va.*   c. 1800
                    Name in script in shaped rectangle
          with spread eagle in circle

   Script capitals in rectangle

ADAM, L.   d. 1731
        Shaded Roman capitals, pellet below in
                shield

ADAMS, DUNLAP   *Philadelphia, Pa.*   w. 1764

ADAMS, PYGAN   *New London, Conn.*   1712–1776

        Roman capitals, pellet between crowned
                in rectangle

        Roman capitals, pellet in rectangle

ADAMS, WILLIAM   *New York, N. Y.*   w. 1833

        Shaded Roman capitals in serrated
                rectangles

ADDISON, GEORGE M.   *Baltimore, Md.*   w. 1804

[3]

SILVERSMITHS AND THEIR MARKS

ADGATE, WILLIAM   *Norwich, Conn.*   1744–1779

ADRIANCE, E.   *St. Louis, Mo.*   c. 1820
[E. ADRIANCE] Small shaded Roman capitals in rectangle
[ST. LOUIS]   Small shaded Roman capitals in rectangle

AIKEN, GEORGE   *Baltimore, Md.*   c. 1815

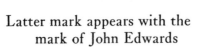   Script in rectangle

AITKEN, JOHN   *Philadelphia, Pa.*   w. 1796

AITKENS, W.   *Baltimore, Md.*   w. 1802

ALCOCK & ALLEN   c. 1810
[*mark*]   Names in capitals in rectangle

ALEXANDER, PHILIP
[*mark*]   Full name incised in large block letters

ALEXANDER, SAMUEL   *Philadelphia, Pa.*   w. 1797
[S. ALEXANDER] Small Roman capitals in rectangle

ALEXANDER, S. & SIMMONS, A.   *Philadelphia, Pa.*   w. 1800
[S. ALEXANDER] Small Roman capitals in rectangles
[A. SIMMONS]   with and without spread eagles

ALFORD, SAMUEL   *Philadelphia, Pa.*   w. 1759

ALFORD, THOMAS   *Philadelphia, Pa.*   w. 1762

ALLEN, JAMES   *Philadelphia, Pa.*   w. 1720

ALLEN, JOEL   *Middletown, Conn.*   1755–1825

ALLEN, JOHN   *Boston, Mass.*   1671–1760

Crude capitals in inverted heart

Crude capitals in quatrefoil

Latter mark appears with the
mark of John Edwards

SILVERSMITHS AND THEIR MARKS

ALLEN, JOHN & EDWARDS, JOHN   *Boston, Mass.*   w. 1699
(*See Allen and Edwards separately*)
[*mark*] IA and IE each in quatrefoil (as above)
These marks also appear with that of D. Parker

ALLEN ROBERT   *Philadelphia, Pa.*   w. 1796

ALLEN, THOMAS   *Boston, Mass.*   w. 1758

ALSTYNE, JERONIMUS   *New York, N. Y.*   w. 1787

AMORY
[AMORY]   Roman capitals in rectangle

ANDERSON, WILLIAM   *New York, N. Y.*   f. 1746

WA   Shaded Roman capitals in rectangle

ANDREW, JOHN   *Salem, Mass.*   1747–1791

I·ANDREW   Shaded Roman capitals in rectangle

ANDREWS, HENRY   *Philadelphia, Pa.*   w. 1796

ANDREWS, H.   *Boston, Mass.*   c. 1830

ANDREWS, J.

J·ANDREWS   Roman capitals in shaped rectangle

ANDREWS, JR.   *Philadelphia, Pa.*   w. 1746

ANTHONY, ISAAC   *Swansea, Mass.*   1690–1773
Newport, R. I.

ANTHONY, JOSEPH   *Philadelphia, Pa.*   w. 1770

J.Anthony   Script in rectangle

J.A   (?)   Shaded Roman capitals in rectangle

J·A   (?)   Shaded Roman capitals in double circle

ANTHONY, JOSEPH & SON   *Philadelphia, Pa.*   w. 1811

J.A
&
I.A
    Shaded Roman capitals, pellet between, in
        square

[5]

ANWYL, KENRICK   *Maryland, Md.*   b. 1748, w. 1775

ARCHIE, JOHN   *New York, N. Y.*   w. 1759

ARMS, T. N.   *Albany, N. Y.*   w. 1849

ARMSTRONG, ALLEN   *Philadelphia, Pa.*   c. 1814

| A.Armstrong |
| Philadelphia |

Roman letters in rectangles

ARMSTRONG, JOHN   *Philadelphia, Pa.*   w. 1811

ARNOLD, THOMAS   *Newport, R. I.*   1739–1828

T·ARNOLD   Small shaded Roman capitals in rectangle

ARNOLD   Shaded Roman capitals in rectangle

TA   Script capitals in rectangle

TA   Large crude capitals in rectangle

TA   (?)   Small shaded capitals in oval

ASHMEAD, WILLIAM   *Philadelphia, Pa.*   w. 1797

ATHERTON, NATHAN, JR.   *Philadelphia, Pa.*   w. 1824

ATTERBURY, J.   *New Haven, Conn.*   w. 1799

AUSTIN, BENJAMIN   *Portsmouth, N. H.*   w. 1775

AUSTIN, EBENEZER   *Hartford, Conn.* b. 1733, w. 1818
    New York, N. Y.

Austin   Shaded Roman letters in rectangle

E·A   Shaded Roman capitals, pellet between in rectangle

AUSTIN, JAMES   *Charlestown, Mass.*   b. 1750

AUSTIN, JOHN   *Hartford, Conn.*   c. 1770

AUSTIN, JOSEPH   *Hartford, Conn.*   bap. 1719

AUSTIN, JOSIAH   *Charlestown, Mass.*   1719–1780

ΓAuſtın   Crude letters in rectangle

J.AUSTIN   Shaded Roman capitals in rectangle

I·A   Crude capitals, pellet between in rectangle

         This mark appears with those of

      Minott   and of   **BOYER**

I·A   Crude capitals pellet between in oval

AUSTIN, NATHANIEL   *Boston, Mass.*   1734–1818

Auſtin   Small Italics in rectangle

N·A   Roman capitals, pellet between in rectangle

AVERY, JOHN   *Preston, Conn.*   1732–1794

IAVERY   Shaded Roman capitals in rectangle

IA   Shaded Roman capitals in rectangle

AVERY, JOHN, JR.   *Preston, Conn.*   1755–1815
          (Son of John)

AVERY, ROBERT STAUNTON   *Preston, Conn.*   1771–1846

AVERY, SAMUEL   *Preston, Conn.*   1760–1836

AVERY, WILLIAM   *Preston, Conn.*   1765–1798

B

BABCOCK, SAMUEL   *Middletown, Conn.*   1788–1857
                 Saybrook, Conn.

BACKUS, DELURINE   *New York, N. Y.*

 **D Backus**   Roman letters in cartouche

D BACKUS   Roman capitals in rectangle

BACON & SMITH   c. 1830
  [mark]   Names in capitals in rectangle

BAIELLE, LEWIS   Baltimore, Md.   w. 1799

BAILEY, BENJAMIN   Boston, Mass.   c. 1800

BAILEY, EDWARD   Maryland, Md.   b. 1753, w. 1774

BAILEY, E. E. AND S. C.   Portland, Me.   c. 1825

| EE & SC BAILEY | Roman capitals in rectangle

BAILEY, HENRY   Boston, Mass.   D. 1808

BAILEY, LORING   Hull, Mass.   1740–1814
                            Hingham, Mass.

| LB | (?)   Shaded Roman capitals in rectangle

BAILEY, R. H.   Woodstock, Vt.   c. 1830

| R.H.BAILEY | Small shaded Roman capitals
| WOODSTOCK | in rectangle

BAILEY, SIMEON A.   New York, N. Y.   w. 1796

BAILEY & CO., E. L.   Claremont, N. H.   c. 1800
  [mark]   Firm name in Roman letters

BAILEY & KITCHEN   Philadelphia, Pa.   w. 1846

BAILY, JOHN   Philadelphia, Pa.   w. 1762

BAKER   Boston, Mass.   w. 1765

BAKER, E.   Conn. (?)   c. 1740–1790

| E.BAKER | Shaded Roman capitals in rectangle

BAKER, GEORGE   Providence, R. I.   w. 1825

| G.BAKER | Roman capitals in rectangle

SILVERSMITHS AND THEIR MARKS

BALCH, EBENEZER	*Hartford, Conn.*	1723–1808
	Wethersfield, Conn.	

E.BALCH   Capitals in rectangle

BALCH & FRYER	*Albany, N. Y.*	w. 1784
BALDWIN, JABEZ	*Salem, Mass.*	w. 1810, d. 1819
	Boston, Mass.	
	(Of Baldwin & Jones)	

BALDWIN   Shaded Roman capitals incised

BALDWIN, JEDEDIAH	*Hanover, N. H.*	c. 1790
BALDWIN & BAKER	*Providence, R. I.*	1817
BALDWIN & JONES	*Boston, Mass.*	c. 1815
	(Jabez Baldwin & John Jones)	

    Shaded Roman capitals in scroll

BALL, JOHN		w. 1770

JOHN BALL.   Italic capitals shaded in cartouche

J·BALL   Crude capitals in rectangle

BALL, S. S.	*Boston, Mass.*	w. 1838
BALL, TRUE M.	*Boston, Mass.*	1815–1890
BALL, W.	*Baltimore, Md.*	w. 1802
BALL, WILLIAM	*Philadelphia, Pa.*	w. 1752

W·Ball   Roman letters in rectangle

WB   Roman capitals in rectangle

BALL   Very small Roman capitals in rectangle

[9]

SILVERSMITHS AND THEIR MARKS

BALL, TOMPKINS & BLACK   *New York, N. Y.*
      (Successors of Marquand & Co.)
[*mark*]   Firm name in small shaded Roman capitals in
      circle

BANCKER, ADRIAN   *New York, N. Y.*   1703–c. 1761

   Roman capitals in oval

   Roman capitals, pellet below in heart

BARD, C. & SON   *Philadelphia, Pa.*   w. 1850

BARD & HOFFMAN   *Philadelphia, Pa.*   w. 1837

BARD & LAMONT   *Philadelphia, Pa.*   w. 1841

BARKER & MUMFORD   *Newport, R. I.*   c. 1825

[BARKER &
  MUMFORD]   Capitals in cartouche

BARNES, ABRAHAM   *Boston, Mass.*   w. 1716

BARRETT, JAMES   *Norwich, Conn.*   c. 1800

  [*JB*]   (?)   Script capitals in rectangle

BARRETT, S.   *Nantucket, Mass.*   c. 1760
                         Providence, R. I. (?)
[S. BARRETT]   Capitals in rectangle

BARROWS, JAMES M.   *Tolland, Conn.*   b. 1809, w. 1832

BARRY, STANDISH   *Baltimore, Md.*   w. 1790

[BARRY]   Shaded Roman capitals in shaped
          rectangle

BARTHOLOMEW, ROSWELL   *Hartford, Conn.*   1781–1830
          (Ward & Bartholomew, 1804)
      (Ward Bartholomew, & Brainard 1809)

[10]

BARTLETT, N.   c. 1760

[N·BARTLETT]   Shaded Roman capitals in
                          rectangle

BARTLETT, SAMUEL   *Concord, Mass.*   c. 1750–1821

[S·BARTLETT]   Shaded Roman capitals in rectangle

[*S.B*]   Script capitals in rectangle

BARTRAM, WILLIAM   *Philadelphia, Pa.*   w. 1769

BASSETT, FRANCIS   *Charlestown, Mass.*   1678–1715

BATEMAN, WILLIAM   *New York, N. Y.*   w. 1774

BATTELS, A. T.   *Utica, N. Y.*   w. 1847

BAYLEY, SIMEON A.   *New York, N. Y.*   w. 1790

[BAYLEY]   Roman capitals in shaped rectangle

[BAYLEY]   Roman capitals in rectangle

BAYLEY & DOUGLAS   *New York, N. Y.*   w. 1798

BAYLY, JOHN   *Philadelphia, Pa.*   w. 1793

BEACH, ISAAC   *New Milford, Conn.*   w. 1788

BEACH, MILES   *Goshen, Conn.*   1742–1828
                        Litchfield, Conn.
                        Hartford, Conn.

[BEACH]   Shaded Roman capitals in rectangle

(MB)   Shaded Roman capitals in oval

BEACH & SANFORD   *Hartford, Conn.*   w. 1785
                   (*See Isaac Sanford*)

BEACH & WARD   *Hartford, Conn.*   w. 1789–1797
                 (*James Beach & Billious Ward*)

BEAL, CALEB   *Hingham, Mass.*   1746–1801

[11]

BEAU, JOHN ANTHONY   *New York, N. Y.*   w. 1770

BECHAM   c. 1740

| BECHAM | Roman capitals in rectangle

BECKER, PHILIP   *Lancaster, Pa.*   w. 1764

[p b]   Capitals in rectangle

BEDFORD, JOHN   *Fishkill, N. Y.*   c. 1780–1834

| *JBedford* | Script in rectangle

BEEBE, STANTON   *Providence, R. I.*   w. 1818
    (Partner of Jabez Gorham)

BEECHER, CLEMENT   *Berlin, Conn.*   1778–1869
    Cheshire, Conn.

[c b]   Capitals in rectangle

BELKNAP, SAMUEL   *Boston, Mass.*   1751–1821

BELL & CO.   c. 1825
    (S. Bell)

[mark]   Name in capitals in rectangle
    with rosettes flanking

BENJAMIN, BARZILLAI   *Milford, Conn.*   1774-1844
    Bridgeport, Conn.
    New Haven, Conn.
    New York, N. Y.

| B.BENJAMIN | Roman capitals in rectangle

| BB | Capitals in rectangle

BENJAMIN, EVERARD   *New Haven, Conn.*   1807–1874
    (Benjamin & Ford)

BENJAMIN, JOHN   *Stratford, Conn.*   1730–1796

(I·B)   Crude capitals, pellet between in oval

SILVERSMITHS AND THEIR MARKS

BENJAMIN, SAMUEL C.   *New Haven, Conn.*   1801–1831
                       (Son of Barzillai)

BENJAMIN, SOLOMON   *Baltimore, Md.*   w. 1817

BENNETT, JAMES   *New York, N. Y.*   w. 1769

BENTLEY, THOMAS   *Boston, Mass.*   c. 1762 – c. 1800

(TB) 🐦   Roman capitals in long oval
          with bird's head flanking

BERARD, ANDREW   *Philadelphia, Pa.*   w. 1797

BESLEY, THAUVET   *New York, N. Y.*   f. 1727

♛̄B   Roman capitals in monogram, crown
     above, incised

BEST, JOSEPH   *Philadelphia, Pa.*   w. 1723

BEVAN, RICHARD   *Baltimore, Md.*   w. 1804

BILLINGS, ANDREW   1743–1808
[A. Billings]   Roman letters in rectangle with
                pseudo hall-marks

BILLINGS, DANIEL   *Preston, Conn.*   w. 1795

(D.Billings)   Script in oval

BILLINGS, JOSEPH   *Pennsylvania* b. c. 1720, w. 1770

BINGHAM, JOHN   *Boston, Mass.*   n. a. f. 1678

BINGLEY   *Conn. (?)*   c. 1790
[BINGLEY]   Roman capitals incised

BLACK, JOHN   *Philadelphia, Pa.*   w. 1819

[J.B] (?)   Roman capitals, pellet between
            in rectangle

[I. BLACK]   Capitals in rectangle

[13]

BLACKMAN, JOHN STARR   *Danbury, Conn.*   1777–1851
            (*Sons J. C. and F. S. were later silversmiths*)

BLAKESLEE, C.   *Vermont (?)*   c. 1820
    [*mark*]   Name in capitals in rectangle
                    with Pure Coin in rectangle

BLAKESLEE, WILLIAM   *Newton, Conn.*   1795–1879
                        (*Son of Zeba*)

BLAKESLEE, ZEBA   *Newton, Conn.*   1768–1825

BLANCHARD, A.   *Lexington, Ky.*   c. 1800

A.BLANCHARD   Large Roman capitals in
                                        long oval

BLISS, I.

BLONDELL, ANTHONY   *Philadelphia, Pa.*   w. 1797

BLOWERS, JOHN   *Boston, Mass.*   1710–1748

Blowers   Semi-script letters in rectangle or oval

BOEHME, CHARLES L.   *Baltimore, Md.*   1804
    [C. BOEHME]   Script in cartouche with eagle displayed

BOELEN, HENDRIK   *New York, N. Y.*   e. 1680, d. 1755
                        (*Son of Jacob*)
Crude capitals in monogram in shield

BOELEN, JACOB   *New York, N. Y.* e. 1680, f. 1698

Crude capitals in shaped shield

(?)   Crude capitals quatrefoil below in shield

(?)   Crude capitals in shield

[14]

BOGARDUS, EVERADUS	*New York, N. Y.*	f. 1698
BOGERT, ALBERT	*New York, N. Y.*	w. 1816
BOGERT, N. J.	*New York, N. Y.*	c. 1820
BOLTON, JAMES	*New York, N. Y.*	w. 1790
BOND, C.		c. 1840

[C. BOND]   Capitals in rectangle

BOND, W.   c. 1765

W Bond   Shaded Roman letters in scalloped
rectangle

BONTECOU, TIMOTHY   *New Haven, Conn.*   1693–1784

T.B.   Capitals incised

BONTECOU, TIMOTHY, JR.   *New Haven, Conn.*   1723–1789

TB   Shaded Roman capitals in oval

BOTSFORD, GIDEON B.   *Woodbury, Conn.*   1776–1866

BOUDINOT, ELIAS   *Philadelphia, Pa.*   1706–1770
(*Father of Elias of Revolutionary fame*)

BOUDINOT   Roman capitals in shaped rectangle

BOURDET, STEPHEN	*New York, N. Y.*	f. 1730
BOUTELLE, JAMES	*Worcester, Mass.*	w. 1783
BOWLER, DANIEL	*Providence, R. I.*	c. 1815
BOWNE, SAMUEL	*New York, N. Y.*	w. 1800

SBOWNE   Shaded Roman capitals in rectangle

BOYCE, GHERARDUS   *New York, N. Y.*   w. 1829

G:BOYCE   Roman capitals shaded in rectangle
with four pellets in rectangle
N.Y.   and N.Y. in rectangle

G.B   Roman capitals, pellet between in rectangle

BOYD, WILLIAM	*Albany, N. Y.*	w. 1810
BOYD & HOYT	*Albany, N. Y.*	w. 1830
BOYD & MULFORD	*Albany, N. Y.*	w. 1840
BOYER, DANIEL	*Boston, Mass.*	c. 1725–1779

BOYER   Roman capitals in rectangle

Boyer   Roman letters in cartouche

DB   Roman capitals in double circle

DB   Roman capitals in oval

BOYER, JAMES	*Boston, Mass.*	1700–1741
BOYLSTON, E.	*Stockbridge, Mass.*	w. 1789
BRACKETT, JEFFREY R.	*Boston, Mass.*	1815–1876

[*marks*] Full name or surname in capitals in rectangle

BRACKETT, CROSBY & BROWN	*Boston, Mass.*	w. 1850
BRADBURY, CAPT. PHINEAS	*New Haven, Conn.*	w. 1779
BRADBURY, THEOPHILUS	*Newburyport, Mass.*	c. 1815

[*mark*] Surname in Roman capitals in rectangle

BRADFORD, CHARLES H.	*Westerly, R. I.*	
BRADBURY & BRO.	*Newburyport, Mass.*	c. 1810
BRADLEY, ABNER	*New Haven, Conn.*	1753–1824

⊕ **A.BRADLEY** ⊕   Shaded Roman capitals in rectangle flanked by quadranted circles

BRADLEY, LUTHER	*New Haven, Conn.*	w. 1798
BRADLEY, PHINEAS	*New Haven, Conn.*	1745–1797

P B   Roman capitals in rectangle

BRADLEY, RICHARD   *Hartford, Conn.*   1787–1867

BRADLEY, ZEBUL   *New Haven, Conn.*   1780–1859
(*See Marcus Merriman & Co. and Merriman & Bradley*)

BRADLEY & MERRIMAN   *New Haven, Conn.*   w. 1826
(*Zebul Bradley, M. Merriman, Jr.*)

 Roman capitals in rectangle, an emblem above

BRADY, WILLIAM V.   *New York, N. Y.*   w. 1835

BRAINARD, CHARLES   *Hartford, Conn.*   1787–1850
(*Of Ward, Bartholomew & Brainard*)

BRAMHALL, S.   *Plymouth Mass. (?),*   c. 1800

[S.BRAMHALL]   Small shaded Roman capitals in rectangle

BRASHER, EPHRAIM   *New York, N. Y.*   D. 1786

(EB)   Shaded Roman capitals in oval

[EB]   Shaded Roman capitals in rectangle

[BRASHER]   Shaded Roman capitals in rectangle
[N.YORK]   with N. YORK in shaded Roman capitals in rectangle

BRASIER, A.

[A·BRASIER]   Roman capitals in rectangle

BREED, JOHN   *Colchester, Conn.*   1752–1803

BREED, W.   *Boston, Mass. (?)*   w. 1750

[WBreed]   Script in rectangle

[WB]   Roman capitals in rectangle

BRENTON, BENJAMIN   *Newport, R. I.*   b. 1710

(BB)   Small Roman capitals in oval

BREVOORT, JOHN   *New York, N. Y.*   f. 1742

IBV (oval)   Crude capitals in oval

(B I V) (trefoil)   Crude capitals in trefoil

BREWER, CHARLES   *Middletown, Conn.*   1778–1860
(*Hart & Brewer, 1800–3, Brewer & Mann, 1803–5*)

C Brewer   Script in shaped rectangle

C.BREWER   Shaded Roman capitals in rectangle

BREWER & MANN   *Middletown, Conn.*   w. 1803
(*See Chas. Brewer*)

BREWSTER, ABEL   *Canterbury, Conn.* b. 1775 – w. 1804
Norwich, Conn.

BRIDGE, JOHN   *Boston, Mass.*   b. 1723

J·BRIDGE   Crude capitals in cartouche

BRIDGE   Roman capitals in cartouche

BRIGDEN, TIMOTHY   *Albany, N. Y.*   w. 1813

BRIGDEN, ZACHARIAH   *Boston, Mass.*   1734–1787

Z·Brigden   Script in cartouche

Z·B   Roman capitals, pellet between, in rectangle

Z B   Roman capitals in rectangle

BRIGDENS, C.

C B (script)   Script capitals in rectangle

C·B   Shaded Roman capitals in rectangle

BRIGHAM, JOHN   n. a. f. 1678

BRIGHT, ANTHONY   *Philadelphia, Pa.*   w. 1740

[18]

SILVERSMITHS AND THEIR MARKS

BRINCKLEY, WILLIAM	*New York, N. Y.*	w. 1804
BRINGHURST	*Maine or N. H.*	late

[*mark*]   Surname in capitals in rectangle

BRINTON, GORDON & QUIRK	*Boston, Mass.*	w. 1780
BROADHURST, SAMUEL	*New York, N. Y.*	f. 1725
BROCK, JOHN	*New York, N. Y.*	w. 1833
BROOKHOUSE, ROBERT	*Salem, Mass.*	1779–1866

Enlaced script capitals in oval

BROWER, S. D.	*Troy, N. Y.*	w. 1834
BROWER, WALTER S.	*Albany, N. Y.*	c. 1850
BROWER & RUSHER	*New York, N. Y.*	c. 1834

B&R   Roman capitals in rectangle with pseudo hall-marks

BROWN, D.	*Philadelphia*	w. 1811

D.BROWN   Shaded Roman capitals in rectangle

BROWN, EBENEZER	*Boston, Mass.*	1773–1816
BROWN, ELNATHAN C.	*Westerly, R. I.*	
BROWN, JOHN	*Philadelphia, Pa.*	w. 1796

J.B   (?) Roman capitals, pellet between, in rectangle

BROWN, S.		c. 1810

S.BROWN   Shaded Roman capitals in serrated rectangle

BROWN, T. J.		c. 1835

T.J.BROWN   Capitals in rectangle

BROWN, WILLIAM	*Albany, N. Y.*	w. 1849

BROWN & HOULTON	*Baltimore, Md.*	c. 1799
BROWN & MANN	*Connecticut*	c. 1805
BROWNE & SEAL	*Philadelphia, Pa.*	c. 1819

[*mark*] Firm name in capitals in scroll with PHILAD^A in rectangle

BRUFF, CHARLES OLIVER	*New York, N. Y.*	w. 1763–1775
BRUFF, JOSEPH	*Philadelphia, Pa.*	w. 1767
BUBE, STANTON	*Providence, R. I. (?)*	c. 1805

(Partner of Geo. C. Clark)

BUEL, ABEL	*New Haven, Conn.*	1742–1825

(Of Buel & Mix)

Shaded Roman capitals in serrated rectangle

Shaded Roman capitals in rayed oval

BUEL, JOHN	*New Haven, Conn.*	1744–1783
BUEL & MIX	*New Haven, Conn.*	w. 1783
BUELL, SAMUEL	*Middletown, Conn.*	w. 1777
	Hartford, Conn.	

Shaded Roman capitals, pellet between, in rectangle

BULL, CALEB	*Hartford, Conn.*	1746–1797
BULL, MARTIN	*Farmington, Conn.*	1744–1825

(Partner of Thos. Lee)

BUMM & SHEPPER	*Philadelphia, Pa.*	w. 1819
BUNKER, BENJAMIN	*Providence, R. I.*	w. 1810
BURDICK, WILLIAM S.	*New Haven, Conn.*	w. 1814

(See Ufford & Burdick)

BURDOCK, NICHOLAS   *Philadelphia, Pa.*   W. 1797

N·B (?) Roman capitals, pellet between, in rectangle

BURGER, JOHN   *New York, N. Y.*   W. 1786

Burger Script in shaped rectangle

N. York Script in rectangle

BURNAP, DANIEL   *E. Windsor, Conn.*   1760–1838
BURNAP, E.

BURNETT, CHARLES A.   *Georgetown, D. C.*   W. 1800

C·A·BURNETT Roman capitals in rectangle

BUROT, ANDREW   *Baltimore, Md.*   W. 1824

BURR, A. C.   c. 1810
[A. C. BURR] Capitals in rectangle

BURR, CHRISTOPHER   *Providence, R. I.*   D. 1824

BURR, EZEKIEL   *Providence, R. I.*   1764–1846

E·BURR Crude capitals in long oval

EB Script capitals in octagon

EB Roman capitals in rectangle

BURR, WILLIAM   *Providence, R. I.*   W. 1792

BURRILL, JOSEPH   *Boston, Mass.*   W. 1823

BURRILL, SAMUEL   *Boston, Mass.*   W. 1733

S:Burrill Semi-script in a cartouche

S:Burrill Semi-script in a rectangle

SB Roman capitals in rectangle

Roman capitals, pellets above,
fleur-de-lys below in heart

BURRILL, THEOPHILUS   *Boston, Mass.*   d. 1739
                                New London, Conn.

BURT, BENJAMIN   *Boston, Mass.*   1729–1805

(BENJAMIN BURT) Italic capitals in cartouche

[B·BURT] Shaded Roman capitals in rectangle

[BURT] Shaded Roman capitals in rectangle

BURT, JOHN   *Boston, Mass.*   1691–1745

(Father of Benjamin, Samuel and William)

(JOHN BURT) Italic capitals in oval

(I·BURT) Italic capitals in cartouche

 Crude capitals crowned, pellet below, in
       shield

(I BURT) Small capitals in oval

BURT, SAMUEL   *Boston, Mass.*   1724–1754

(SAMUEL BURT.) Shaded Italic capitals in cartouche

BURT, WILLIAM   *Boston, Mass.*   1726–1752

(W.BURT) Roman capitals in oval

BUSHNELL, PHINEAS   *Guilford, Conn.*   1741–1836

BUSSEY, BENJ.   *Dedham, Mass.*   1757–1842
                   (Founder of Bussey Institute)

BB   Capitals in rectangle

BUSSEY, THOS.	*Baltimore, Md.*	w. 1799
BUTLER, JAMES	*Boston, Mass.*	1713–1776

J.BUTLER   Shaded Roman capitals in rectangle

IB   Roman capitals in rectangle

BUTLER, JOHN	*Falmouth (Portland), Me.*	w. 1763
BUTLER, N.	*Utica, N. Y.*	w. 1803
BUTLER & McCARTHY	*Philadelphia, Pa.*	w. 1850
BUZELL, J. L.		c. 1750

J.L.BUZELL   Shaded Roman capitals in rectangle

BYRNE, JAMES	*New York, N. Y.*	w. 1790

J.Byrne   Italics in cartouche

C

CADY, SAMUEL	*New York, N. Y.*	w. 1796
CADY & BACKUS	*New York, N. Y.*	w. 1796
CALDER & CO.	*Troy, N. Y.*	w. 1830
CALLENDER, BENJAMIN	*Boston, Mass.*	w. 1784
CAMERON, ALEXANDER	*Albany, N. Y.*	w. 1813
CAMOIN	*Philadelphia, Pa.*	w. 1797
CAMPBELL, R.	*Baltimore, Md.*	w. 1824
CAMPBELL, R. & A.	*Baltimore, Md.*	w. 1850
CAMPBELL, WILLIAM	*Philadelphia, Pa.*	w. 1765
CANDEE, LEWIS BURTON	*Woodbury, Conn.*	1806–1861

CANFIELD, SAMUEL	*Middletown, Conn.* w. 1780–1807
	Lansingburg, N. Y.
	Scanticoke, N. Y.

CANFIELD Capitals in long oval

CANFIELD BROS. & CO.	*Baltimore, Md.*	w. 1850
CANFIELD & FOOT	*Middletown, Conn.*	w. 1795
CANN, JOHN	*New York, N. Y.*	w. 1836
CANT, GODFREY	*New York, N. Y.*	w. 1796
CARALIN, PIERCE	*New York, N. Y.*	w. 1804
CARGILL		
CARIO, MICHAEL	*Philadelphia, Pa.*	w. 1736
CARIO, WILLIAM		b. 1721

W.CARIO Shaded Roman capitals in scalloped rectangle

W.CARIO Shaded Roman capitals in shaped rectangle

| CARLETON & CO. | | c. 1800 |

CARLETON✠C? Shaded Roman capitals in rectangle

CARNAN, JOHN	*Philadelphia, Pa.*	w. 1771
CARPENTER, CHARLES	*Boston, Mass.*	w. 1807
CARPENTER, JOSEPH	*Norwich, Conn.*	1747–1804

IC (?) Shaded Roman capitals in rectangle

CARRINGTON, DANIEL NOBLE	*Danbury, Conn.*	w. 1793
(Partner of E. Mygatt and N. Taylor)		
CARROL, JAMES	*Albany, N. Y.*	w. 1834
CARSON, DAVID	*Albany, N. Y.*	w. 1849

[24]

CARSON, THOMAS   *Albany, N. Y.*   w. 1813
                     (*Carson &. Hall*)

CARSON & HALL   *Albany, N. Y.*   w. 1813

CARY, LEWIS   *Boston, Mass.*   1798–1834

Shaded Roman capitals in scalloped scroll ending in rosettes

CASE, GEORGE   *East Hartford, Conn.*   w. 1779

CASEY, GIDEON   *South Kingston, R. I.*   w. 1753

CASEY, SAMUEL   *Newport, R. I.*   c. 1724–c. 1773

Roman capitals in rectangle

Roman capitals in oval

CASTON, FRANCOISE   *New York, N. Y.*   w. 1804

CHALMERS, I.   *Annapolis, Md.*   w. 1780
        (*Issued the Annapolis shilling in 1783*)

CHAMPLIN, JOHN   *New London, Conn.*   1745–1800

CHANDLESS, WILLIAM   *New York, N. Y.*   w. 1846
     [mark]   Capital C with pseudo hall-marks

CHAPIN, AARON   *Hartford, Conn.*   1753–1838

CHAPMAN, HENRY   *Carolina*   b. 1744, w. 1774

CHARTERS, JAMES   *New York, N. Y.*   w. 1844

CHARTERS, CANN & DUNN   *New York, N. Y.*   w. 1850

CHASLEY   *Boston, Mass.*   w. 1764

CHAT. LE SIEUR   *New York, N. Y.*   w. 1790

CHAUDRON'S & RASCH   *Philadelphia, Pa.* (?)   c. 1820
   [CHAUDRON'S & RASCH]   Small shaded Roman
                       capitals in scroll

CHAUDRON & CO.

   [CHAUDRON]   Capitals in scroll

CHELIUS   c. 1840

CHENE, DANIEL   *New York, N. Y.*   w. 1786

CHILDS, GEORGE K.   *Philadelphia, Pa.*   w. 1837

CHITRY, P.   *New York, N. Y.*   w. 1816

    (P.Chitry)   Roman letters in long oval

    [P.Chitry]   Roman letters in rectangle

CHITTENDEN, EBENEZER   *New Haven, Conn.*   1726–1812
                      Guilford, Conn.
                      Madison, Conn.

    (EC)   Roman capitals in oval

    [E.CHITTENDEN]   Roman capitals in rectangle

    [EC]   Roman capitals in rectangle

CHURCH, JOSEPH   *Hartford, Conn.*   1794–1876
   (Of Church & Rogers, also worked with Jacob Sargeant)

CHURCH & ROGERS   *Hartford, Conn.*   D. 1828
           (See Joseph Church)

CHURCHILL, JESSE   *Boston, Mass.*   1773–1819

    [I·CHURCHILL]   Shaded Roman capitals in rectangle

    [CHURCHILL]   Small shaded Roman capitals in rectangle

    [CHURCHILL]   Large shaded Roman capitals in
                     rectangle

CHURCHILL & TREADWELL   *Boston, Mass.*   w. 1815

    [Churchill Treadwell]   Shaded Roman letters in rectangle

CLAPP & RIKER   *New York, N. Y.*   w. 1805

CLARK, C. & G.   *Boston, Mass.*   w. 1833

CLARK, CHARLES   *New Haven, Conn.* w. 1798

CLARK, GEORGE C. *Providence, R. I.* w. 1813
     (Partner of Jabez Gorham)

| G.C.CLARK | Large Roman capitals in rectangle

CLARK, I.   *Boston or Salem, Mass.* w. 1754

| ICLARK | Crude capitals in rectangle

| I.CLARK | Crude capitals in rectangle, with pellet

| CLARK | Crude capitals in rectangle

CLARK, I. & H.   *Portsmouth, N. H.*

| I·&H·CLARK | Small capitals in rectangle

CLARK, JOSEPH   *Danbury, Conn.* w. 1791, d. 1821
     (Brother of Thomas)

| JC | Roman capitals in rectangle

CLARK, JOSEPH   *Portsmouth, N. H.* w. 1800

CLARK, LEVI   *Norwalk, Conn.* 1801–1875

CLARK, METCALF   *Boston, Mass.*   w. 1835

CLARK, PETER G.   *New Haven, Conn.* w. 1810

CLARK, SAMUEL   *Boston, Mass.* 1659–1705

CLARK, THOMAS   *Boston, Mass.*   d. 1783
    (Older brother of Joseph of Danbury

| T.Clark | Roman letters in shaped oval

CLARK, WILLIAM   *New Milford, Conn.* 1750–1798

| WC | Roman capitals in rectangle

[27]

SILVERSMITHS AND THEIR MARKS

CLARK & ANTHONY

| CLARK &ANTHONY | Capitals in rectangle |

CLARKE, JONATHAN   *Newport, R. I.*   w. 1734

G.Clarke   Script in long oval

IC   Large crude capitals in rectangle

J·CLARKE   Shaded Roman capitals in rectangle

CLEMMONS, ISAAC   *Boston, Mass.*   c. 1775

CLEVELAND, AARON   *Norwich, Conn.*   w. 1820

AC   Capitals in hexagon

CLEVELAND, WILLIAM   *Norwich, Conn.*   1770–1737
                          Salem, Mass.
(*Of Trott & Cleveland, Grandsire of Grover Cleveland*)

Cleveland   Roman letters in rectangle

WC   Roman letters in rectangle

CLEVELAND & POST   *New London Conn. (?)*   c. 1799

C&P   Roman capitals in rectangle

COBB, EPHRAIM   *Boston, Mass.*   1708–1775
                          Plymouth, Mass.

ECobb   Italic letters in rectangle

EC   Roman capitals in rectangle

COBURN, JOHN   *Boston, Mass.*   1725–1803

J.COBURN   Roman capitals in rectangle

IC   Roman capitals in rectangle

COE & UPTON, & H. L. SAWYER   *New York, N. Y.* c. 1840

[COE ᗉUPTON] [N] [Y] Roman capitals in rectangles
[H.L.SAWYER]

CODDINGTON, JOHN   *Newport, R. I.*   1690–1743

     Crude capitals in emblem

CODNER, JOHN   *Boston, Mass.*   1754–1782

COEN, DANIEL   *New York, N. Y.*   w. 1787

COGSWELL, H.   *Boston, Mass. (?)*   c. 1750

[H.COGSWELL] Roman letters in rectangle

COIT, THOMAS C.   *Norwich, Conn.*   1791–1841
(See Coit and Mansfield)

COIT & MANSFIELD   *Norwich, Conn.*   w. 1816
(See E. H. Mansfield)

COLE, ALBERT   *New York, N. Y.*   w. 1850

COLE, JOHN   *Boston, Mass.*   n. a. f. 1686

COLEMAN, NATHANIEL   *Burlington, N. J.*   w. 1790

[N.COLEMAN] Roman capitals in rectangle

COLES, A.   late

     Superimposed capitals in diamond flanked
with head and eagle

COLES, JOHN A.   *New York, N. Y. (?)*   late

Ⓒ Capital in octagon with pseudo hall-marks

COLEY, SIMEON   *New York, N. Y.*   w. 1767

SILVERSMITHS AND THEIR MARKS

COLLINS, ARNOLD   *Newport, R. I.*   w. 1690, d. 1735

AC   Crude capitals in shield

AC   Roman capitals in heart

COLWELL & LAWRENCE   *Albany, N. Y.*   w. 1850

COLEY, WILLIAM   *New York, N. Y.*   w. 1816

W Coley   Script in shaped oval

CONEY, JOHN   *Boston, Mass.*   1655–1722

IC +   Crude capitals, cross below in heart

IC   Crude capitals, crowned, coney below in shield

IC   (?)   Crude capitals in oval

IC   (?)   Small crude capitals in rectangle

CONNELL, M.   *Philadelphia, Pa.* (?)   c. 1800

M:CONNELL   Shaded Roman capitals in rectangle

CONNING, J.   *Philadelphia, Pa.* (?)   c. 1800
[J. CONNING]   Roman capitals in rectangle

CONNOR, J. H.   *Norwalk, Conn.*

J.H.CONNOR   Roman capitals in rectangle

CONYERS, JOSEPH   *Boston, Mass.*   c. 1708

CONYERS, RICHARD   *Boston, Mass.*   d. 1708

COOK, J.   *Portland, Me.* (?)   c. 1820

J.COOK   Roman capitals in rectangle

SILVERSMITHS AND THEIR MARKS

COOKE, JOHN   *New York, N. Y.*   w. 1804

COOKE, JOSEPH   *Philadelphia, Pa.*   w. 1789

COOLIDGE, JOSEPH, JR.   *Boston, Mass.*   w. 1770

(*Coolidge*)   Script in cartouche

[J. C.] (?)   Capitals in rectangle

COOPER, B. & J.   c. 1830

[B. & J. / COOPER]   Capitals incised

COOPER, F. W.   *New York, N. Y.*   w. 1840

[*mark*] Woman's head, C (old English), lion

COOPER, G.   c. 1800

G.COOPER   Very small Roman capitals incised

COPP, JOS.   *New London, Conn.*   w. 1776

COPP, NATHANIEL P.   *Troy, N. Y.*   w. 1834

CORNELISON, CORNELIUS   *New York, N. Y.*   f. 1712

CORNELL, WALTER   *Providence R. I. (?),*   c. 1800

[CORNELL]   Shaded Roman capitals in scalloped
          rectangle

COVERLEY, THOMAS   *Newburyport, Mass.* c. 1750–1800

[T·COVERLY]   Roman capitals in rectangle

COWELL, WILLIAM   *Boston, Mass.*   1682–1736

[W:Cowell]   Italics in a cartouche

[WC]   Shaded Roman capitals, star and two
          pellets above, pellet below in
          shaped shield

(WC)   Shaded Roman capitals in oval

[WC]   Shaded Roman capitals in rectangle

[31]

COWELL, WILLIAM, JR.   *Boston, Mass.*   1713–1761

This maker's marks have not yet been distinguished from those of his father, and it is probable that some given previously belong to him. No. 1 above was used by him in 1753, and by his father in 1727. No. 2 was probably not used by him, and the other two appear to have been used by both

COX, J. & I.   *New York, N. Y.*   c. 1840

J&ICOX   Roman capitals in rectangle
N.YORK   Roman capitals in rectangle

J&I COX   Roman capitals incised

CRANDELL, BENJAMIN   *Providence, R. I.*   D. 1824

CRANSTON, SAMUEL   *Newport, R. I.*   1659–1727

CRAWFORD, JOHN   *New York, N. Y.*   w. 1815

J.CRAWFORD   Roman capitals in rectangle

J.Crawford   Script in rectangle

CREW, J. T.   *Albany, N. Y.*   w. 1849

CROSBY, JONATHAN   *Boston, Mass.*   b. 1743, w. 1796

JC   Roman capitals in double circle

CROSBY, SAMUEL T.   *Boston, Mass.*   w. 1850

CROSS   *Boston, Mass.*   w. 1695

CROUCKESHANKS, ALEXANDER   *Boston, Mass.*   w. 1768

CUMMING, DAVID B.   *Philadelphia, Pa.*   w. 1811

CURRY, JOHN   *Philadelphia, Pa.*   w. 1831

CURRY & PRESTON   *Philadelphia, Pa.*   w. 1830

CURRY&PRESTON   Roman capitals in serrated rectangle

[32]

CURTIS, JOEL	*Wolcott, Conn.*	b. 1786
	Cairo, N. Y.	
CURTIS, LEWIS	*Farmington, Conn.*	1774–1845

L·CURTIS   Roman capitals in rectangle

CURTISS, DANIEL	*Woodbury, Conn.*	1801–1878

(*Of Curtiss & Candee; Curtiss, Candee & Stiles; Curtiss & Stiles*)

CURTISS, CANDEE & STILES	*Woodbury, Conn.*	c. 1820
CUTLER, A.	*Boston, Mass.*	c. 1820
[*mark*]	Name in capitals in rectangle	
CUTLER, J. N.	*Albany, N. Y.*	w. 1849
CUTLER, RICHARD	*New Haven, Conn.*	1736–1810

(*Cutler, Silliman, Ward & Co., Richard Cutler & Sons*)

CUTLER, RICHARD, JR.	*New Haven, Conn.*	1774–1811
CUTLER, WILLIAM	*New Haven, Conn.*	1785–1817
	(*Son of Richard*)	

CUTLER, SILLIMAN, WARD & CO.   *New Haven, Conn.* w. 1767
(*Richard Cutler, Hezekiah Silliman, Ambrose Ward*)

D

DABRALL, WILLSON	*Carolinas*	b. 1749, w. 1774
DAGGET, HENRY	*New Haven, Conn.*	1741–1830
DALLY & HALSEY	*New York, N. Y.*	w. 1787
DANA, P.		c. 1795
[P. Dana]	Roman letters in rectangle	
DANE, THOMAS	*Boston, Mass.*	c. 1724–c. 1796

T.DANE   Shaded Italic capitals in oval

T DANE   Shaded Roman capitals in cartouche

[33]

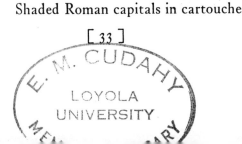

DAVENPORT, SAMUEL	*Milton, Mass.*	1720–1793
DAVERNE, JOHN	*Baltimore, Md.*	w. 1799
DAVID, JOHN	*New York, N. Y.*	1736–1798
	Philadelphia, Pa.	
	(Son of Peter)	

[I·DAVID]   Roman capitals in rectangle

[JD]   Roman capitals in small oval

[ID]   Crude capitals in small oval

DAVID, LEWIS A.	*Philadelphia, Pa.*	w. 1837
DAVID, PETER	*Philadelphia, Pa.*	w. 1738
DAVIS, E.	*Newburyport, Mass.*	
		w. 1775, d. 1781

[EDavis]   Script in rectangle.

[ED]   Shaded Roman capitals in rectangle
Both marks usually accompanied by
a lion passant

DAVIS, JOSHUA G.	*Boston, Mass.*	w. 1796

[ID AVIS]   Capitals in a serrated rectangle

DAVIS, SAMUEL	*Plymouth, Mass.*	w. 1801
DAVIS, T. A.	*Boston, Mass.*	w. 1824

[T.A.DAVIS]   Shaded Roman capitals in rectangle

DAVIS, WILLIAM	*Boston, Mass.*	w. 1823
DAVIS & BABBITT	*Providence, R. I.*	c. 1815
DAVIS & BROWN		

[DAVIS & BROWN]   Shaded Roman capitals in
rectangle

DAVIS, PALMER & CO.   *Boston, Mass.*   c. 1841

(Davis Palmer &Cº)   Small shaded Roman letters or capitals
BO STON   in flat oval with shaded Roman
Pure Silver Coin   capitals in rectangle
Italics in rectangle

DAVIS, WATSON & CO.   *Boston, Mass.*   c. 1820

DAVIS WATSON &CO   Roman capitals in rectangle

DAVISON, BARZILLAI   *Norwich, Conn.*   1740–1828

DAVISON, C.   *New York, N. Y. (?)*   late

C DAVISON   Capitals in oval

DAVY, ADAM   *Philadelphia, Pa.*   w. 1796

DAWS, R.   c. 1800

R·DAWS   Roman capitals incised

DAWES, WILLIAM   *Boston, Mass.*   1719–1802

DAWKINS, HENRY   *New York, N. Y.*   w. 1754–1776
Philadelphia, Pa.

DAWSON, JOHN   *New York, N. Y.*   w. 1767

DELANO, JABEZ   *New Bedford, Mass.*   1763–1848

DEMILT   c. 1800

DEMILT   Shaded Roman capitals in rectangle

DEMMOCK, JOHN   *Boston, Mass.*   w. 1798

DENISE, JOHN & TUNIS   *New York, N. Y.*   w. 1798

J&TD   Capitals with Phœnix's head;
and wheat sheaf in three
separate rectangles

DENISON, T.   c. 1790

T.DENISON   Shaded Roman capitals in rectangle

DENNIS, EBENEZER   *Hartford, Conn.*   b. 1753

[35]

DENNIS, GEORGE, JR.   *Norwich, Conn.*   b. 1753
(*Brother of E. Dennis*)

DE PEYSTER, WILLIAM   *New York, N. Y.*   f. 1733

DE REMIER, PETER   *New York, N. Y.*   f. 1769

(PDR)   Roman capitals in flat oval

DE REMIER & MEAD   *Ithaca, N. Y.*   w. 1831

DESHON, DANIEL   *New London, Conn.*   1697–1781

DEVERELL, JOHN   *Boston, Mass.*   c. 1764–1813

[Deverell]   Small Roman letters in rectangle

DEWING, FRANCIS   *Boston, Mass.*   b. c. 1716

DEXTER, JOHN   *Dedham, Mass.*   1735–1800
Marlboro, Mass.

DEXTER, MINERVA   *Middletown, Conn.*   b. 1785

DICKERSON, JOHN   *Morristown, N. J.*   w. 1778
Philadelphia, Pa.

DICKINSON, ANSON   *Litchfield Conn.*   c. 1800
New York, N. Y.

DILLING, D.   c. 1760
[D. DILLING]   Roman capitals

DIXON, A.   c. 1800

DIXWELL, BASIL   *Boston, Mass.*   1711–1746
(*Son of John*)

DIXWELL, JOHN   *Boston, Mass.*   1680–1725
(*Son of the Regicide*)

(ID)   Roman capitals in oval

(ID)   Very small Roman capitals in oval

DOANE, JOSHUA   *Providence, R. I.*   d. 1753

[DOANE]   Roman capitals in cartouche

DOANE, JOHN	*Boston, Mass.*	1733–1801
DOBBS	*New York, N. Y.*	w. 1788
DODGE, EZRA	*New London, Conn.*	1766–1798
DODGE, NEHEMIAH	*Providence, R. I.*	w. 1794

[N·DODGE]   Thin unshaded crude capitals in serrated rectangle

DODGE, SERIL   *Providence, R. I.* w. 1795, d. 1802

☆   [S·DODGE] ☆   Shaded Roman capitals in serrated rectangle, a star incised at either end

DOLE, D. N.   c. 1780

[D·N·DOLE]   Shaded Roman capitals in rectangle

DOLE, E. G.   c. 1820

[EGDole]   Roman letters in rectangle

DOLER, DANIEL	*Boston, Mass.*	w. 1765
DONALDSON, JOHN W.	*Boston, Mass.*	w. 1823
DONOVAN, W.		c. 1780

[W DONOVAN]   Roman capitals in rectangle

DOOLITTLE, AMOS   *New Haven, Conn.*   1754–1832

(AD)   Thin Roman capitals in oval

DOOLITTLE, ENOS	*Hartford, Conn.*	w. 1781
DORSEY, JOSHUA	*Philadelphia, Pa.*	w. 1797

[I·DORSEY]   Shaded Roman capitals in rectangle

DOUGLAS, CANTWELL	*Baltimore, Md.*	w. 1799
DOUGLAS, ROBERT	*New London, Conn.*	1740–1776

(RD)   Monogram in shield

(RD)   Monogram in wedge

DOWIG, GEORGE   *Philadelphia, Pa.*   w. 1765

GD (?)   Roman capitals in oval

DOWIG, GEORGE   *Baltimore, Md.*   w. 1789
    (Perhaps the same as previous name)

DOWNES, J.   *Philadelphia, Pa. (?)* c. 1770

J.Downes   Roman letters in shaped rectangle

DOWNING, G. R.   *New York, N. Y.* w. 1810 (?)
    (Possibly of Downing & Phelps)

GRD   Capitals in rectangle with anchor,
    star and head

DOWNING & PHELPS   *New York, N. Y. (?)* w. 1810

D&P   Roman capitals in rectangle

DREWRY, GEORGE   *Philadelphia, Pa.*   w. 1763

DROWN, T. P.   c. 1800

T P DROWN   Shaded Roman capitals in rectangle

DROWNE, BENJAMIN   *Portsmouth, N. H.* w. 1800

DROWNE, SAMUEL   *Portsmouth, N. H.* 1749–1815
    (Nephew of Shem)

S×Drowne   Script in rectangle with indented ends

S×D   Crude capitals, × between, in rectangle

DROWNE, SHEM   *Boston, Mass.*   1683–1774

DUBOIS, A.   *Philadelphia, Pa.*   w. 1797

ADUBOIS   Roman capitals in rectangle

DUBOIS, JOSEPH   *New York, N. Y.* w. 1790

J·DUBOIS   Thin shaded Roman capitals in
    rectangle

[38]

SILVERSMITHS AND THEIR MARKS

DUBOIS, T. D.   c. 1780

T·D·DUBOIS Shaded Roman capitals in rectangle
with sheaf of wheat in rectangle

T·D·D ▰ ▰ Shaded Roman capitals in rectangle
with sheaves of wheat in rectangles

DUCHÉ, RENE ROCK   *New York, N. Y.*   w. 1804

DUFFEE   c. 1785
[DUFFEE]   In capitals

DUFFIELD, EDWARD   *Philadelphia, Pa.*   w. 1756

DUMMER, JEREMIAH   *Boston, Mass.*   1645–1718

(I·D ✠) Roman capitals, pellet between,
fleur-de-lys below in heart

DU MORTE, JOHN   *Philadelphia, Pa.*   w. 1796

DUMOUTET, I. B.   *Philadelphia, Pa.*   w. 1797

(DUMOUTET) Roman capitals in scroll

DUNHAM, R.

R DUNHAM   Capitals incised

DUNKERLY, JOSEPH (?)   *Boston, Mass.*   w. 1787

DUNLEVEY, ROBERT   *Philadelphia, Pa.*   w. 1787

DUNN, CARY   *New York, N. Y.*   f. 1765

(C·DUNN) Roman capitals, initials larger, in
flattened oval

DUPUY, DANIEL   *New York, N. Y.*   1719–1807

DD Roman capitals in rectangle

(D·DUPUY) Small shaded Roman capitals
in rectangle

[39]

DUPUY, DANIEL, JR.	*Philadelphia, Pa.*	w. 1796
DURAND, CYRUS	*Newark, N. J.*	1787–1868
DUSENBERRY		c. 1800
[DUSENBERRY]	Capitals incised	
DUVALIER		c. 1800

DUVALIER Shaded Roman capitals in rectangle

DUYCKINCK, D.	*New York, N. Y.* (?)	c. 1790
[D. DUYCKINCK]	Capitals in rectangle	
DWIGHT, TIMOTHY	*Boston, Mass.*	1654–1691

TD Roman capitals, six pellets in rose form below, in heart

E

EAMES, JOSHUA	*Boston, Mass.*	d. 1722
EASTON, JAMES	*Nantucket, Mass.*	w. 1828
	(Apprentice of Hadwen's)	
EASTON, J., 2D	*Nantucket, Mass.*	w. 1847
[J. Easton, 2d]	Roman letters in rectangle	
[Nantucket Pure Coin]		
EASTON & SANFORD	*Nantucket, Mass.*	w. 1837
[Easton & Sanford]	Roman letters in rectangle	
EAYERS, THOMAS STEVENS	*Boston, Mass.*	c. 1760–c. 1803

EAYRES Roman capitals in rectangle

EDDY & BARROWS	*Tollard, Conn.*	w. 1832
EDMECHAT, CLAUDE	*New York, N. Y.*	w. 1790
EDWARDS, ABRAHAM	*Ashby, Mass.*	w. 1763
	(Son of Samuel of Natick)	

EDWARDS, ANDREW   *Boston, Mass.*   1763–1798

EDWARDS, CALVIN   *Ashby, Mass.*   b. 1763
         (Son of Samuel of Natick)

EDWARDS, JOHN   *Boston, Mass.*   c. 1670–1746

 Crude capitals in plain quatrefoil

 Crude capitals in quatrefoil with four
     projections

 Roman capitals in two semi-circles with
     two projections

 Crude capitals crowned, fleur-de-lys
     below in shield

EDWARDS, JOSEPH   *Boston, Mass.*   1737–1783
         (Grandson of John)

IEdwards   Script with Roman capital initials in
     rectangle

I·E   Roman capitals, with and without pellet

I E   between, in rectangle

EDWARDS, SAMUEL   *Boston, Mass.*   1705–1762
         (Son of John)

 Crude capitals crowned, pellet between,
     fleur-de-lys below, in shaped shield

 Crude capitals crowned, pellet between,
     in shaped shield

EDWARDS, SAMUEL   *Natick, Mass.*   1726–1783

EDWARDS, THOMAS   *Boston, Mass.*   1701–1755
           (*Son of John*)

T·Edwards	Script with Roman capital initials, pellet between, in rectangle (and in oval)
TE	Roman capitals in rectangle
T·E (crowned in shield)	Crude capitals crowned in shield

EDWARDS, THOMAS   *New York, N. Y.*   f. 1731

ELDERKIN, ALFRED   *Windham, Conn.*   1759–1833

ELDERKIN, ELISHA   *Killingworth, Conn.*   1753–1822
           New Haven, Conn.

ELLESON, PETER   *New York, N. Y.*   w. 1796

ELLIOT, H.
     [H. ELLIOT]   Capitals in scroll

ELLIOTT, JOHN A.   *Sharon, Conn.*   b. 1788 (?)

ELLSWORTH, DAVID   *Windsor, Conn.*   1742–1821

EMBREE

EMBREE	Large Roman capitals in rectangle

EMERY, STEPHEN   *Boston, Mass.*   c. 1752–1801

S·Emery·	Shaded Roman letters in cartouche
SE	Roman capitals in rectangle
Emery	Roman letters in cartouche
SE (?)	Roman capitals in oval
S·Emery	Shaded Roman letters in shaped rectangle
S·Emery	Shaded Roman letters in rectangle
S·E	Roman capitals, pellet between, in rectangle

EMERY, THOMAS KNOX   *Boston, Mass.*   c. 1781–1815
(*Son of Stephen*)

T·K·EMERY.	Large capitals in rectangle
T·K·E	Small shaded Roman capitals in rectangle
T·Emery	Roman letters in cartouche

EMERY & CO.   *Boston, Mass.*   w. 1798

ENGLAND, WILLIAM   *Philadelphia, Pa.*   f. 1718

ENSIGN   after 1800

ENSIGN	Roman capitals in rectangle with pseudo hall-marks

EOFF, GARRETT   *New York, N. Y.*   c. 1785–1850

G.EOFF	Capitals in rectangle
G.Eoff	Letters in rectangle

EOFF & CONNER   *New York, N. Y.*   w. 1833

EOFF & HOWELL   *Philadelphia, Pa. (?)*

EOFF & PHYFE   *New York, N. Y.*   w. 1850

E&P	Shaded Roman capitals in rectangle

EOFF & SHEPHERD   *New York, N. Y. (?)*   late

E&S	Capitals in rectangle with pseudo hall-marks

EPPS, ELLERY   *Boston, Mass.*   D. 1808

ERWIN, JOHN   *Baltimore, Md.*   w. 1817

ETTER, B.   c. 1780

B·ETTER	Thin Roman capitals in rectangle with sheaf of wheat

ETTING, BENJAMIN	*New York, N. Y.*	f. 1769
EVANS, HENRY	*New York, N. Y. (?)*	late

HENRY EVANS   Capitals in rectangle with pseudo hall-marks

EVANS, JOHN	*New York, N. Y.*	w. 1816
EVANS, ROBERT	*Boston, Mass.*	c. 1768–1812

R.EVANS   Shaded Roman capitals in rectangle

EVANS   Shaded Italic capitals in rectangle, with serrated top and scalloped bottom

R E   Roman capitals in rectangle

R·E   Roman capitals, pellet between, in rectangle

EVERTSON, JOHN	*Albany, N. Y.*	w. 1813
EWAN, J.	*Charleston, S. C.*	c. 1800

J.EWAN   Roman capitals in scalloped rectangle

F

FABER, WILLIAM	*Philadelphia, Pa.*	w. 1831
FABER & HOOVER	*Philadelphia, Pa.*	w. 1837
FAIRCHILD, JOSEPH	*New Haven, Conn.*	D. 1824
FAIRCHILD, ROBERT	*Stratford, Conn.*	1703–1794

R·FAIRCHILD   Roman capitals in rectangle

R×F   Roman capitals, × between, in cartouche

FAIRMAN, GIDEON	*New London, Conn.*	1774–1827
	Albany, N. Y.	
	Philadelphia, Pa.	

[44]

FARIS, CHARLES   Boston, Mass.   c. 1790

(C⁵Faris)   Script in long oval

(ChaˢFaris)   Script in long oval

FARLEY, CHARLES   Ipswich, Mass.   w. 1812
                              Portland, Me.

(C.FARLEY)   Shaded Roman capitals in rectangle with
                  spread eagle in oval at each end

(FARLEY)   Shaded Roman capitals in rectangle with
                  spread eagle in oval at each end

FARNAM, C. H.

(C H FARNAM)   Capitals in rectangle

FARNAM, HENRY   Boston, Mass.   b. 1773

(H·FARNAM)   Small Roman capitals in rectangle

FARNAM, RUFUS   Boston, Mass.   b. c. 1771

(R.FARNAM)   Shaded Roman capitals in rectangle

FARNAM, R. &. H.   Boston, Mass.   w. 1807

(R&H·FARNAM)   Shaded Roman capitals in rectangle

FARNAM, THOMAS   after 1800

[TH: FARNAM]   Capitals in rectangle

FARNAM & WARD   Connecticut   w. 1810

(FARNAM &WARD)   Roman capitals in rectangle

FARNSWORTH, J. C.

[mark]   Name incised

FARRINGTON, JOHN   Boston, Mass.   w. 1833

FARRINGTON & HUNNEWELL   Boston, Mass.   w. 1835

(F&H)   Capitals in rectangle

[45]

FELLOWS   *Newport R. I. (?)*   c. 1800

[J.Fenno]   Shaded Roman capitals in long oval

FELLOWS & GREEN   *Maine (?)*   c. 1825

[FELLOWS & GREEN]   Capitals in rectangle

FELT, J. S.   *Portland, Me.*   c. 1825

[J. S. FELT]   Capitals in rectangle

FENNO, J.   c. 1825

[FELLOWS]   Small slightly shaded Roman letters in oval

FEURT, PETER   *New York, N. Y.*   d. 1737
                               Boston, Mass.

PF   Heavy Roman capitals, crowned, fleur-de-lys below in shield

FIELDING, GEORGE   *New York, N. Y.*   f. 1731

GF (?)   Capitals in oval

FIFIELD, JOHN S.   *Westerly, R. I.*

FINCH, HIRAM   *Albany, N. Y.*   w. 1840

FINLAYSON, HENRY   *Savannah, Ga. (?)*   w. 1770

FIRENG, J. P.   *Burlington, N. J.*   c. 1830

FISHER, T.   *Baltimore, Md. (?)*   c. 1765

[T.Fisher]   Italics in wedge

FITCH, ALLEN   *New Haven, Conn.*   b. 1785
                   (Fitch & Hobart)

FITCH & HOBART   *New Haven, Conn.*   w. 1813

FLAGG, JOSIAH   *Boston, Mass.*   c. 1713–1741

FLAGG, JOSIAH, JR.   *Boston, Mass.*   b. 1738

FLETCHER, THOMAS   *Boston, Mass.*   c. 1810
                        Philadelphia, Pa.   c. 1830

[T. FLETCHER]   Roman capitals
[PHILAD.   ]

FLETCHER & GARDNER   *Boston, Mass.*   w. 1810
                        Philadelphia, Pa.
    (*Thos. Fletcher and Sidney Gardner*)

| F.&G. | Roman capitals in rectangle |

FLING, GEORGE   *Philadelphia, Pa.*   w. 1749

FLOTT, LEWIS   *Baltimore, Md.*   w. 1817

FOLSOM, JOHN   *Albany, N. Y.*   f. 1781

FOOT, WILLIAM   *East Haddam, Conn.*   b. 1772

FORBES, ABRAHAM G.   *New York, N. Y.*   w. 1769

FORBES, B. G.   *New York, N. Y.*   w. 1833

FORBES, COLIN V. G.   *New York, N. Y.*   w. 1816

FORBES, G.   *New York, N. Y.*   w. 1816

| G.FORBES | Shaded Roman capitals in rectangle |

FORBES, I. W.   *New York, N. Y.*   w. 1805

| I W FORBES | Roman capitals in rectangle, sometimes with pseudo hall marks |

| IWF ★ NY | Small Roman capitals in rectangles, star between |

FORBES, W.   *New York, N. Y.*   w. 1839

| W.FORBES | Roman capitals in rectangle |

FORBES, WILLIAM G.   *New York, N. Y.* f. 1773, w. 1803

| W.G Forbes | Script in rectangle (1803) |

| W.FORBES | Large Roman capitals in rectangle (1792) Sometimes with pseudo hall-marks |

FORD, JAMES M.

FORD, SAMUEL   *Philadelphia, Pa.*   w. 1797

FORMAN, BERWIN B.   *Albany, N. Y.*   w. 1813

FORREST, ALEX.	*Baltimore, Md.*	w. 1802
FOSTER, ABRAHAM	*Boston, Mass.*	b. 1728, w. 1800
FOSTER, GEORGE B.	*Salem, Mass.*	w. 1838
	Boston, Mass.	

[*mark*] Full name in rectangle with "Coin" in Gothic

FOSTER, JOSEPH	*Boston, Mass.*	1760–1839

[FOSTER] Shaded Roman capitals in rectangle

[I·FOSTER] Shaded Roman capitals in rectangle

FOSTER, N. & T.	*Newburyport, Mass. (?)*	c. 1800
FOSTER, SAMUEL	*Boston, Mass.*	1676–1702
FOSTER, T.	*Newburyport, Mass. (?)*	c. 1800

[T.FOSTER] Capitals in rectangle

FOURNIQUET, LEWIS	*New York, N. Y.*	1796

[*Fourniquet*] Italics in cartouche

FRANCIS, JULIUS C.	*Middletown, Conn.*	1785–1862

(Of Hughes & Francis in 1807–1809)

FRANCIS, N.	*New York, N. Y.*	w. 1805–1816

[N FRANCIS] Roman capitals in rectangle with eagle in square with serrated top

FRANCISCUS, GEORGE	*Baltimore, Md.*	w. 1817
FRASER, WILLIAM	*Philadelphia, Pa.*	w. 1738
FREEBORN, N.		c. 1800

[N·FREEBORN] Shaded Roman capitals in serrated rectangle

FREEMANS, J. M. & Co.		c. 1800

[J.M.FREEMANS & Co] Small shaded Roman capitals in rectangle

FROBISHER, BENJAMIN C.   *Boston, Mass.*   1792–1862

[B.C.Frobisher]   Shaded Roman letters in rectangle

FROST & MUMFORD   *Providence, R. I.*   c. 1810

FROTHINGHAM, EBENEZER *Boston, Mass.*   1756–1814

FRYER, JOHN W.   *Albany, N. Y.*   w. 1813

FUETER, DANIEL CHRISTIAN *New York, N. Y.*   w. 1754

(D C F)   Roman capitals in oval

(N YORK)   Italic capitals in shaped oval

FUETER, DAVID   *New York, N. Y.*   w. 1789

FUETER, LEWIS   *New York, N. Y.*   w. 1770

FURER   *New York, N. Y.*   w. 1759

G

GADLEY & JOHNSON   *Albany, N. Y.*   c. 1849

GALE, I. L.   c. 1820
   [I. L. GALE] Capitals in rectangle
   [I. L. G.]   Capitals in rectangle

GALE, JOHN   *New York, N. Y.*   w. 1816

[J.GALE]   Roman capitals in rectangle

GALE, WILLIAM   *New York, N. Y.*   w. 1821
   [W. G.]   With pseudo hall-marks

GALE, WM. & SON   *New York, N. Y.*   c. 1850
   [W. G. & S.] or [G. & S.]   With pseudo hall-marks

GALE & HAYDEN   *New York, N. Y.*   w. 1848
   [G. & H.]   With pseudo hall-marks

GALE & MOSELEY   *New York, N. Y. (?)*   late

GALE & WILLIS   *New York, N. Y. (?)*   late

GALE, WOOD & HUGHES   *New York, N. Y.*   w. 1833

[G.W&H]   Roman capitals between a head and eagle in circles

GULLUP, CHRISTOPHER   *No. Groton, Conn.*   1764–1849

GARDEN, FRANCIS   *Boston, Mass.*   w. 1745

GARDINER, B.   *New York, N. Y.*   w. 1829

[B. GARDINER]
[NEW YORK]   Roman capitals on curved band with pseudo hall-marks

GARDNER, JOHN   *New London, Conn.*   1734–1776

[J·GARDNER]   Shaded Roman capitals in rectangle

[IG]   Capitals in rectangle

GARDNER, SIDNEY   *Boston, Mass.*   c. 1810
(Of Fletcher & Gardner)

GARNSEY

GARRETT, P.   *Philadelphia, Pa.*   w. 1811

[P.GARRETT]   Capitals in rectangle

GASKINS, J.   c. 1760

[J·GASKINS]   Roman capitals in shaped rectangle

GAY, NATHANIEL   *Boston, Mass.*   1643–1713

GEE, JOSEPH   *Philadelphia, Pa.*   w. 1788

GEFFROY, NICHOLAS   *Newport, R. I.*   1761–1839

[N GEFFROY.]   Shaded Roman capitals in scalloped rectangle

[GEFFROY]   Shaded Roman capitals in scalloped rectangle

GELSTON, G. S.   *New York, N. Y.*   w. 1833

GELSTON, GEO. P.   *Boston, Mass.*   w. 1830
      (Of Walcott & Gelston)

GELSTON, HENRY   *Boston, Mass.*   w. 1828

GELSTON, HUGH   *Boston, Mass.*   w. 1816

GELSTON, MALTBY   *Boston, Mass.*   d. 1828
      (Of Walcott & Gelston)

GELSTON & CO.   *New York, N. Y.*   w. 1836
  [GELSTON & CO NEW YORK]   In capitals

GELSTON & TREADWELL   *New York, N. Y.* (?)   late
  [*mark*]   Name in capitals in rectangle

GELSTON, LADD & CO.   *New York, N. Y.*   late

[GELSTON LADD & CO]   Capitals in rectangle

GEORGEON, BERNARD   *Philadelphia, Pa.*   w. 1797

GERMON, G. D.   *Philadelphia, Pa.*   w. 1819

GERMON, JOHN   *Philadelphia, Pa.*   w. 1788

GERRISH, TIMOTHY   *Portsmouth, N. H.*   1753–1813

[*J.Gerrish*]   Script in rectangle

[GERRISH]   Capitals in engrailed rectangle

[T G]   (?)   Capitals in rectangle

GHISELIN, CESAR   *Philadelphia, Pa.*   d. 1733

⊠ [CG] ⊠   Crude capitals in rectangle flanked
      by outlined stars

(CG)   Crude capitals in heart

GHISELIN, WILLIAM   *Philadelphia, Pa.*   w. 1751

GIBBS, DANIEL   *Boston, Mass.*   w. 1716

GIBBS, JOHN   *Providence, R. I.*   d. 1797

[J GIBBS]   Capitals in rectangle

GIBNEY, M.   *New York, N. Y.* (?)

[51]

GIFFING, C.   *New York, N. Y.*   late
[C. GIFFING N. Y.]   Capitals in rectangle with pseudo
                 hall-marks

GILBERT, SAMUEL   *Hebron, Conn.*   w. 1798
SG   Capitals in rectangle

GILBERT, WILLIAM   *New York, N. Y.*   w. 1783
Wᵐ Gilbert   Semi-script in rectangle
WG   Roman capitals in rectangle

GILBERT & CUNNINGHAM   *New York, N. Y.*   w. 1839

GILL, CALEB   *Hingham, Mass.*   1774–1855

GILL, LEAVITT   *Hingham, Mass.*   1789–1854

GILLEY, PETER   *Philadelphia, Pa.*   w. 1797

GILMAN, BENJ. CLARK   *Exeter, N. H.*   1763–1835
BCG   Roman capitals in rectangle

GILMAN, JOHN WARD   *Exeter, N. H.*   1771–1823
[I. W. G.]   Capitals incised

GIUDE, THOMAS   *New York, N. Y.* b. 1751, w. 1774

GIVEN, A.   *Albany, N. Y.*   w. 1849

GOELET, PHILIP   *New York, N. Y.* b. 1701, f. 1731
PG   Crude capitals in oval

GOLDTHWAITE, JOSEPH   *Boston, Mass.*   1706–1780

Crude capitals crowned, fleur-de-lys
below in shield

Crude capitals crowned, fleur-de-lys
below in quatrefoil

GOODE, L.

[L. GOODE]   Capitals in rectangle

GOODHUE, JOHN   *Salem, Mass.*   w. 1840 (?)

[J.GOODHUE]   Capitals in rectangle

GOODING, HENRY   *Boston, Mass.*   w. 1833

[GOODING]   Small shaded Roman capitals in rectangle

GOODING, JOSIAH   c. 1810

[Josiah Gooding]   Small Roman letters in rectangle

[Joys Building]   Smaller Italic letters in long oval

GOODWIN, ALLYN   *Hartford, Conn.*   1797–1869

GOODWIN, BENJAMIN   *Boston, Mass.*   w. 1756

[B.Goodwin]   Shaded Roman letters in rectangle
     with triangular dots between initials

GOODWIN, H. & A.   *Hartford, Conn.*   D. 1825
(*The Brothers Horace and Allyn*)

GOODWIN, HORACE   *Hartford, Conn.*   1787–1864

GOODWIN, RALPH   *Hartford, Conn.*   1793–1866

GOODWIN & DODD   *Hartford, Conn.*   w. 1812

GOOKIN, DANIEL   *Boston, Mass.*   b. 1682
(*Apprenticed to Dummer in 1696*)

GORDON, A. & J.   *New York, N. Y.*   w. 1798

GORDON, ANDREW   *New York, N. Y.*   w. 1796

[GORDON]   Shaded Roman capitals in serrated rectangle
(*This mark may be that of Jas. Gordon*)

GORDON, JAMES   *New York, N. Y.*   w. 1796

GORDON & CO.   *Boston, Mass.*   w. 1849

GORHAM, J. & SON   *Providence, R. I.*   w. 1841

GORHAM, JABEZ	*Providence, R. I.*	b. 1792
GORHAM, JOHN	*New Haven, Conn.*	w. 1814
GORHAM, JOHN	*Providence, R. I.*	b. 1820
GORHAM, MILES	*New Haven, Conn.*	1757–1847

M.G — Capitals in rectangle

M.GORHAM — Capitals in rectangle

GORHAM, RICHARD	*New Haven, Conn.*	1775–1841

(Of Shethar & Gorham, 1804)

GORHAM & WEBSTER	*Providence, R. I.*	w. 1831
[mark]	Name in script in rectangle or scroll	
GOUGH, JAMES	*New York, N. Y.*	w. 1769
GOWEN, WILLIAM	*Charlestown, Mass.*	1749–c. 1803
	Medford, Mass.	

W·GOWEN — Shaded Roman capitals in rectangle

WG — Shaded Roman capitals in rectangle

GRAHAM, DANIEL	*West Suffield, Conn.*	b. 1764
GRANT, THOMAS	*Marblehead, Mass.*	1731–1804

T·GRANT — Roman capitals in rectangle

GRANT, WILLIAM	*Marblehead, Mass.*	1766–1809
GRANT, WILLIAM	*Philadelphia, Pa.*	w. 1796
GRAY, CHARLES	*Maryland*	b. 1749, w. 1774
GRAY, G.		c. 1825

G.GRAY — Shaded Roman capitals in serrated rectangle

GRAY, JOHN	*Boston, Mass.*	1692–1720
	New London, Conn.	

I.G (?) — Capitals in rectangle

GRAY, ROBERT   *Portsmouth, N. H.*   d. 1850

[ROB? GRAY] Small shaded Roman capitals in rectangle
with extremely small scallops

[R·Gray] Thin unshaded Roman letters in rectangle

GRAY, SAMUEL   *Boston, Mass.*   1684–1713
New London, Conn.
(Brother of John)

[S:GRAY] Roman capitals in rectangle

[GRAY] (?) Roman capitals in rectangle

GRAY, SAMUEL   *Boston, Mass.*   b. 1710

GRAY & LIBBY   late

GREEN, BARTHOLOMEW   *Boston, Mass.*   b. 1697

GREEN, BENJAMIN   *Boston, Mass.*   1712–1776

[B:GREEN] Shaded Roman capitals in rectangle

GREENE, RUFUS   *Boston, Mass.*   1707–1777

[R·GREENE] Shaded Roman capitals in waved
rectangle

[R.GREENE] Shaded Roman capitals in shaped
rectangle

[R·G] Shaded Roman capitals, pellet between,
in cartouche

[R·G] Shaded Roman capitals, pellet between,
in shaped rectangle

[RG] (?) Small capitals in rectangle

[RG] (?) Capitals crowned in shield

GREENE, WILLIAM & CO.   *Providence, R. I.*   c. 1815

[55]

GREENLEAF, DAVID	*Bolton, Mass.*	1737–1800
	Norwich, Conn.	
	Hartford, Conn.	

[D.Greenleaf] Roman letters in rectangle

GREENLEAF, DAVID. JR.	*Hartford, Conn.*	1765–1835

[GREENLEAF] Shaded Roman letters in scalloped
rectangle

GREENLEAF, JOSEPH	*New London, Conn.*	1778–1798
GREENOUGH, DANIEL	*Newcastle, N. H.*	w. 1714
GRIFFIN, ISAIAH		w. 1802
GRIFFITH, DAVID	*Boston, Mass.*	D. 1798
GRIGG, WILLIAM	*New York, N. Y.* f. 1765, w. 1779

[Grigg] Script in shaped rectangle

GRIGNON, BENJAMINE	*Boston, Mass.*	n. a. f. 1685
GRIGNON, RENÉ (Capt.)	*Norwich, Conn.*	d. 1715

[RG] Roman capitals crowned, stag courant
below, in a shield

GRISWOLD, GILBERT	*Middletown, Conn.*	c. 1810
	Portland, Me.	
GUILLE, NOAH	*Boston, Mass.*	w. 1701
GUIRNA, ANTHONY	*Philadelphia, Pa.*	w. 1796
GUNN, ENOS	*Waterbury, Conn.*	b. 1770
[E. GUNN]	Capitals in rectangle	
GURLEY, WILLIAM	*Norwich, Conn.*	b. 1764

[W.G] Roman capitals in rectangle

GURNEE, B. & S.	*New York, N. Y.*	w. 1833

H

HACKLE, WILLIAM	*Philadelphia, Pa.*	w. 1766
HADDOCK, HENRY	*Boston, Mass.*	c. 1830
HADDOCK & ANDREWS	*Boston, Mass.*	w. 1838
HADDOCK, LINCOLN & FOSS	*Boston, Mass.*	w. 1865

[*mark*]   Firm name in small Roman capitals incised

HADWEN, WILLIAM	*Providence, R. I.*	w. 1813–1820
	Nantucket, Mass.	

(*Partner of Jabez Gorham*)

HALL, A. B.

HALL, ABIJAH	*Albany, N. Y.*	w. 1813
HALL, CHARLES	*Lancaster, Pa.*	w. 1765
HALL, DAVID	*Philadelphia, Pa.*	w. 1765
HALL, DREW	*New York, N. Y.*	w. 1789
HALL, GREEN	*Albany, N. Y.*	d. 1863

(*Of Carson & Hall*)

HALL, JOSEPH	*Albany, N. Y.*	f. 1781

[I. HALL] (?)   Capitals in rectangle

HALL & BROWER	*Albany, N. Y.*	w. 1853
HALL & HEWSON	*Albany, N. Y.*	w. 1819
HALL, HEWSON & BROWER	*Albany, N. Y.*	w. 1845
HALL, HEWSON & CO.	*Albany, N. Y.*	w. 1836
HALL, HEWSON & MERRIFIELD	*Albany, N. Y.*	w. 1840
HALLAM, JOHN	*New London, Conn.*	1752–1800
HALSEY, JABEZ	*New York, N. Y.*	1762–1820

[I·HALSEY]   Roman capitals in rectangle

HALSTED, BENJAMIN   *New York, N. Y.*   w. 1764–1783
                           Philadelphia, Pa.
                           Newark, N. J.

[*Halsted*]   Script in irregular shape

HALSTRICK, JOSEPH   *Boston, Mass.*   1815–1886

HALSTRICK, WM. S.

HAM, GEORGE   *Portsmouth, N. H.*   w. 1810

HAMERSLY, THOMAS   *New York, N. Y.*   w. 1756

[TH]   Script capitals in oval

[T·H]   Shaded Roman capitals, pellet
               between, in rectangle

HAMILL, J.   *New York, N. Y.*   c. 1810
[J. HAMILL, N. Y.]   Capitals in rectangle

HAMILTON, JAMES   *Annapolis, Md.*   w. 1766

HAMLIN, CYRUS   *Portland, Me.*   1810–1900

HAMLIN, WILLIAM   *Providence, R. I.*   b. 1772
                           Middletown, Conn.

HANCOCK, JOHN   *Charlestown, Mass.*   b. 1732
                           Providence, R. I.

[J·HANCOCK]   Shaded Roman capitals in rectangle

HANKS, BENJAMIN   *Windham, Conn.*   1738–1810
                           Litchfield, Conn.
                           Ashford, Conn.

HANNAH, W. W.   *Albany, N. Y. (?)*   c. 1850
[mark]   Name incised in capitals with pseudo hall-marks

HANNERS, GEORGE   *Boston, Mass.*   c. 1696–1740

[G·HANNERS]   Italic capitals in rectangle

[GH]   Crude capitals crowned, pellet below
              in shield

[58]

HANNERS, GEORGE, JR.	*Boston, Mass.*	1721–1760
HANSELL, ROBERT	*Boston, Mass.*	c. 1823
HARDING, C. H.		late
[*mark*]	Name in capitals incised	
HARDING, NEWELL	*Haverhill, Mass.*	1799–1862
	Boston, Mass.	

[N.Harding]   Very small Italic letters in scroll

[NHarding]   Very small unshaded Roman letters
in rectangle

HARDING, N. & CO.	*Boston, Mass.*	c. 1860
HARDY, STEPHEN	*Portsmouth, N. H.*	1781 1843
	(Apprentice of Revere's and Wm. Simes')	

(HARDY)   Capitals in long octagon

[HARDY]   Roman letters in rectangle

HARLAND, THOMAS	*England*	1735–1807
	Norwich, Conn.	

[HARLAND]   In rectangle or scroll between profile
and eagle displayed

HARLAND, THOMAS, JR.	*Norwich, Conn.*	1781–1806
HARMON, REUBEN	*New York, N. Y.*	w. 1787
HARRIS & STANWOOD	*Boston, Mass.*	w. 1845
[*mark*]	Name in capitals in rectangle	
HARRIS & WILCOX	*Troy, N. Y.*	w. 1844
HART, ELIPHAZ	*Norwich, Conn.*	1789–1866

[E.HART]   Shaded Roman capitals in rectangle

[EH]   Shaded Roman capitals in rectangle

HART, JUDAH   *Middletown, Conn.*   1777–1824
                        Norwich, Conn.
(Hart and Brewer, 1800; Hart and Bliss, 1803; Hart and
                   Wilcox, 1805)

J.HART   Roman capitals in rectangle

J Hart   Script in rectangle

HART & BLISS   *Middletown, Conn.*   w. 1803

HART & BREWER   *Middletown, Conn.*   w. 1800

HART & SMITH   late
[*mark*]   Name in rectangle with pseudo hall-marks

HART & WILCOX   *Norwich, Conn.*   w. 1805
        (Judah Hart and Alran Wilcox)

☞   H✦W   Capitals with index hand, each in rectangle

HARWOOD

HAR
WOOD   Capitals in square

HASCY, ALEXANDER   *Albany, N. Y.*   w. 1849

HASCY, NELSON   *Albany, N. Y.*   w. 1849

HASKELL, BARNABAS   *Boston, Mass.*   w. 1833

HASTIER, JOHN   *New York, N. Y.*   f. 1726

IH   Roman capitals in heart

J·H   Roman capitals, pellet between, in rectangle

IH   Roman capitals in rectangle

HASTIER, MARGUERIETTE   *New York, N. Y.*   w. 1771

HASTINGS   c. 1830
    [*mark*]   Name in capitals in rectangle with eagle

HAYDEN & GREGG	*Charleston, S. C.*	w. 1832–1840
HAYES, W.	*Conn. (?)*	c. 1780

[W·Hayes]   Roman letters in rectangle

[WH]   Large Roman capitals in rectangle

HAYES & COTTON	*Newark, N. J.*	w. 1831
HAYS, ANDREW	*New York, N. Y.*	f. 1769
HAYS & MYERS	*New York, N. Y.* *Newport, R. I.* (*Meyer Myers*)	c. 1765

[H&M]   Shaded Roman capitals in rectangle

HEALY, SAMUEL	*Boston, Mass.*	d. 1773
HEARN, R. [R. HEARN]	Capitals in rectangle	
HEATH, JOHN	*New York, N. Y.*	f. 1761

(I·HEATH)   Capitals in flat oval

HEBBERD, H.	*New York, N. Y.*	w. 1847
HEDGES [*mark*]	Name in capitals in rectangle	c. 1830
HELME	*South Kingston, R. I.*	

[HELME]   Capitals in wedge

HEMING, THOMAS	*New York, N. Y. (?)*	c. 1764
HEMPSTED, E.		w. 1820
HENCHMAN, DANIEL	*Boston, Mass.*	1730–1775

[Henchman]   Shaded Roman letters in rectangle

[D·H]   Shaded Roman capitals, pellet between, in rectangle

SILVERSMITHS AND THEIR MARKS

HENDRICKS, AHASUERUS   *New York, N. Y.*

m. before 1679, f. 1698

Roman capital monogram in oval

HEQUEMBURG, CHARLES, JR.   *New Haven, Conn.*   1760–1851

HERBERT, LAWRENCE   *Philadelphia, Pa.*   w. 1748

HERON, ISAAC   *New York, N. Y.*   w. 1768

HEUGHAN, JOHN   *Schenectady, N. Y.*   w. 1772

HEWES, ABRAM   *Boston, Mass.*   w. 1823

HEWS, A., JR.   *Boston, Mass.*   c. 1850
  [*mark*]   Name in capitals incised

HEWSON, JOHN D.   *Albany, N. Y.*   d. 1862

HEYER, W. B.   *New York, N. Y.*   1798–1827

Sometimes with   H&N   or   J.GALE

W.B.Heyer   Semi-script in rectangle

HIAMS, MOSES   *Philadelphia, Pa.* b. 1751, w. 1775

HIGGINS, ABRAHAM   *Eastham, Mass.*   1738–1763
     (*Apprentice of Moody Russell (?)*)

HILLER, BENJAMIN   *Boston, Mass.*   b. 1687, w. 1739

Crude capitals in cartouche

Crude capitals, two crescents below, in shaped shield

HILLER, JOSEPH   *Boston, Mass.*   1721–1758
     (*Son of Benjamin*)

HILLER, JOSEPH (MAJOR)   *Salem, Mass.*   1748–1814
     (*Grandson of Benjamin*)

HILLDRUP, THOMAS   *Hartford, Conn.*   d. c. 1795

HINSDALE, EPAPHRAS   *New York, N. Y.*   w. 1796

HINSDALE, H.   *New York, N. Y.*   c. 1831

HITCHBORN, SAMUEL   *Boston, Mass.*   1752–1828

HITCHCOCK, ELIAKIM   *Cheshire, Conn.*   1726–1788
     New Haven, Conn.
[E H] (?)   Capitals in rectangle

HOBART, JOSHUA   *New Haven, Conn.*   w. 1813
     (*Of Fitch & Hobart*)

[J·HOBART]   Capitals in rectangle

HOBBS, NATHAN   *Boston, Mass.*   1792–1868

[HOBBS]   Small Roman capitals in rectangle

[N.Hobbs]   Small Roman letters in rectangle

HODGMAN, T.

HODSDON

HOLLAND, LITTLETON   *Baltimore, Md.*   c. 1804

[HOLLAND]   Small shaded Roman capitals in rectangle with pseudo hall-marks

HOLLINGSHEAD, WILLIAM   *Philadelphia, Pa.*   w. 1762

HOLMES, ISRAEL   *Greenwich, Conn.*   1768–1802
     Waterbury, Conn.

HOLTON, DAVID   *Baltimore, Md.*   w. 1804

HOLYOKE, EDWARD   *Boston, Mass.*   w. 1817
[HOLYOKE]   Capitals in rectangle

HOMES, WILLIAM, SR.   *Boston, Mass.*   1717–1783

W·HOmes	Mixed Roman letters in rectangle
HOMES	Shaded Italic capitals in rectangle
HOMES	Unshaded Italic capitals in rectangle
W·H	Shaded Roman capitals, pellet between, in rectangle
W·H	Small Roman capitals, pellet between, in rectangle
WH	Small Roman capitals, no pellet between, in rectangle

HOMES, WILLIAM, JR.   *Boston, Mass.*   1742–1825

A comparison of the inscriptions on Homes' silver indicates that father and son probably used some of the same marks, the identification of the maker depending, therefore, upon the period of the piece. The W H marks appear to occur more frequently on the son's silver, while the marks containing the name seem to be found on the father's pieces

HOOD & TOBEY	*Albany, N. Y.*	w. 1849
HOOKEY, WILLIAM	*Newport, R. I.*	d. 1812
HOPKINS, JESSE	*Waterbury, Conn.*	b. 1766
HOPKINS, JOSEPH	*Waterbury, Conn.*	1730–1801
HOPKINS, STEPHEN	*Waterbury, Conn.*	1721–1796
HORN, E. B.	*Boston, Mass.*	w. 1847
HOTCHKISS, HEZEKIAH	*New Haven, Conn.*	d. 1761

HOTCHKISS & SCHROEDER

H❦S	Capitals incised

HOUGH, SAMUEL   *Boston, Mass.*   1675–1717

SH	Capitals in rectangle

SILVERSMITHS AND THEIR MARKS

HOULTON, JOHN   Philadelphia, Pa.   w. 1797

HOVY
  [Hovy]   Roman letters

HOW, DAVID   Boston, Mass. b. c. 1745, w. 1805
                            Castine, Maine

HOWARD, ABRAM   Salem, Mass.   w. 1810

HOWARD, WILLIAM   Boston, Mass.   D. 1823

HOWE, OTIS   Boston, Mass.   1788–1825
                            Portsmouth, N. H.

HOWELL, G. W.   c. 1790

[G.W.Howell]   Script in rectangle

HOWELL, JAMES   Philadelphia, Pa.   w. 1811

[J.Howell]   Semi-script in shaped rectangle

HOYT, GEORGE B.   Albany or Troy, N. Y.   c. 1830
  [GEO. B. HOYT]   With pseudo hall-marks

HUERTIN, WILLIAM   New York, N. Y. f. 1731, d. 1771

(WH) (?)   Roman capitals in oval

[WH]   Roman capitals in rectangle

HUGES, CHRISTOPHER & Co.   Baltimore, Md.   w. 1773

HUGHES, EDMUND   Hampton, Conn.   w. 1804–1806
                            Middletown, Conn.

(Of Ward & Hughes, 1805; Hughes & Bliss, 1806; Hughes
            & Francis 1807–1809)

HUGHES, HENRY   Maryland   b. 1756, w. 1774
                        [65]

HULL, JOHN   *England*   1624–1683
                             Boston, Mass.

  Crude capitals, fleur-de-lys below, in heart

  Crude capitals, rose above, in superim-
                      posed circles

  Crude capitals, rose above, in rectangle
                      surmounted by circle

HULL & SANDERSON   *Boston, Mass.*   w. 1652

   John Hull and Robert Sanderson
                                           each placed his individual
                                           mark on pieces made by the
                        firm. These marks will be
                                           found listed under their
                                           separate names. While prob-
                        ably other combinations may
                                           have been used, the ones noted
                                           at present are given at left

HULL & SANGER   after 1800

HUMPHREY, RICHARD   *Philadelphia, Pa.*   w. 1771

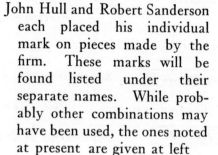   Script in shaped oval

[RH]   (?)   Capitals in rectangle

HUMPHREYS, THOMAS   *Philadelphia, Pa.*   w. 1814

HUNT, EDWARD   *Philadelphia, Pa.*   f. 1718

HUNTER, DANIEL   *Newport, R. I.*   c. 1785

HUNTINGTON, PHILIP   *Norwich, Conn.*   1770–1825

   [PH]   (?)   Capitals in rectangle

HUNTINGTON, ROSWELL   *Norwich, Conn.*   b. 1763

HUNTINGTON, S.   *Maine (?)*   late
   [mark]   Name in rectangle

SILVERSMITHS AND THEIR MARKS

Hurd, Benjamin   *Roxbury, Mass.*   1739–1781

[B↑H] (?)   Crude capitals, arrow between, in rectangle

Hurd, Jacob   *Boston, Mass.*   1702–1758

[Jacob Hurd]   Roman letters in cartouche

(IHURD)   Sloping Roman capitals in cartouche

(Hurd)   Semi script with sloping Roman initial letter, in oval

[HURD]   Small, shaded Roman capitals, in rectangle

[HURD]   Thin large Roman capitals in rectangle

[Hurd]   Small Roman letters in flat-top cartouche

(Hurd)   Small Roman letters in cartouche

[I·H] (?)   Roman capitals, pellet between, in cartouche

Hurd, Nathaniel   *Boston, Mass.*   1729–1777
(Son of Jacob)

[N·Hurd]   Shaded Roman letters in rectangle

[N·Hurd]   Very small letters in cartouche

[N·Hurd]   Small Roman letters in shaped rectangle

Hurlbeart, Philip   *Philadelphia, Pa.*   d. 1764

Hurst, Henry   *Boston, Mass.*   c. 1665–1717

HH   Roman letters in shield

Hurtin & Burgi   *Boundbrook, N. J.*   w. 1766

HUSBAND, JOHN   *Philadelphia, Pa.*   w. 1796

HUSTON, JAMES   *Baltimore, Md.*   w. 1799

HUTCHINSON, J.

HUTT, JOHN   *New York, N. Y.*   w. 1774

HUTTON, GEORGE   *Albany, N. Y.*   w. 1796
            (Partner of Isaac)

HUTTON, ISAAC   *Albany, N. Y.*   1767–1855

| HUTTON | Shaded Roman capitals in rectangle with eagle in circle |

| HUTTON ALBANY | Roman capitals in divided rectangle |

HUTTON, JOHN   *New York, N. Y.*   f. 1720

| H·I | Roman capitals, pellet between, in rectangle |

HUTTON, JOHN S.   *New York, N. Y.*   1684–1792
            Philadelphia, Pa.

HYDE   *Newport, R. I.*   c. 1730 (?)

| HYDE | Roman capitals in rectangle |

HYDE & GOODRICH   *New Orleans, La.*   w. 1830

HYDE & NEVINS   *New York, N. Y.*   w. 1798
            (Associated with W. B. Heyer)

| Hyde&Nevins | Shaded Roman letters in rectangle |

I

IVES, DAVID

IVES, L.

ILSLEY   c. 1830
   [mark] Name in capitals in engrailed rectangle
   [mark] Name in large capitals in serrated rectangle

IVERS, B.   c. 1800
  B·IVERS   Small shaded Roman capitals, initials
              larger, in serrated rectangle

J

JACKSON, JAMES   *Maryland*   b. 1756

JACKSON, JOHN   *New York, N. Y.*   1632–1736
  JACKSON   Crude capitals in rectangle

JACKSON, JOSEPH   *Baltimore, Md.*   w. 1804

JACOBS, A.   *New York, N. Y.*   c. 1800
   [mark] Name in capitals in rectangle
   [mark] Name in capitals incised

JACOBS, GEORGE   *Baltimore, Md.*   w. 1802

JACOBS, MOSES   *Philadelphia, Pa.* b. 1753, w. 1775

JARVIS, MUNSON   *Stamford, Conn.*   1742–1825
  M·J   Roman capitals, pellet between, in rectangle

JENCKES, JOHN C.   *Providence, R. I.*   w. 1795
  J JENCKES   Capitals incised

JENKINS, JOHN   *Philadelphia, Pa.*   w. 1796

JENNINGS, JACOB   *Norwalk, Conn.*   1729–1817

JENNINGS, JACOB, JR.   *Norwalk, Conn.*   b. 1779

JESSE, DAVID   *Boston, Mass.*   1670–1705
  D·I   Shaded Roman capitals, circle above,
           pellet below, in a circle
  D·I   Shaded Roman capitals, pellet
           between, in oval

JOHNSON, C.   Albany, N. Y.   w. 1825
[mark]   Name in rectangle with pseudo hall-marks

JOHNSON, M. W.   Albany, N. Y.   w. 1815

JOHNSON, SAMUEL   New York, N. Y.   w. 1783

[S·J] (?)   Crude capitals, pellet between, in rectangle

JOHNSON, WILLIAM   Boston, Mass.   w. 1799

JOHNSON & GODLEY   Albany, N. Y.   w. 1847

JOHNSON & REAT   Portland, Me. (?)   c. 1810

[JOHNSON ⅋ REAT]   Capitals in shaped rectangle
                              with eagle

JOHONNOT, WILLIAM   Middletown, Conn.   1766–1849
                              Windsor, Vt.

JONES, GEORGE B.   Boston, Mass.   c. 1815–1875

JONES, JOHN   Boston, Mass.   c. 1810
                    (Of Baldwin & Jones)

[J.JONES]   Roman capitals in rectangle

JONES, JOHN B.   Boston, Mass.   1782–1854

[J.B.JONES]
[PURE COIN]   Capitals in two rectangles

JONES, WM.   Marblehead, Mass.   1694–1730

[W·I]   Crude capitals in rectangle

JONES, JOHN B. & Co.   Boston, Mass.   w. 1838

JONES & WARD   Boston, Mass.   c. 1815

JONES, BALL & Co.   Boston, Mass.   w. 1852
[mark]   Firm name incised in capitals

JONES, BALL & POOR   Boston, Mass.   w. 1846
[mark]   Firm name in capitals incised

JONES, LOW & BALL   *Boston, Mass.*   w. 1839
[*mark*]   Firm name in capitals in rectangle

JUDAH   *New York, N. Y.*   w. 1774

K

KAY, AM   *Boston, Mass.*   c. 1725
[AK]   Crude capitals in rectangle

KEELER, JOSEPH   *Norwalk, Conn.*   1786–1824
[IK]   Capitals in rectangle

KEELER, T.   c. 1800
[T.KEELER]   Shaded Roman capitals in rectangle

KEITH, TIMOTHY   *Boston, Mass.*   c. 1800
[T — KEITH]   Capitals in rectangle

KELLEY, ALLEN   *Providence, R. I.*   c. 1810

KELLEY, E. G. & J. H.   *Providence, R. I.*   c. 1820

KELLY, GRAEL   *Boston, Mass.*   w. 1823

KENDAL, CHARLES   *New York, N. Y.*   w. 1787

KENNEY, THOMAS   *Norwich, Conn.*   c. 1825
                         (*See Thomas Kinney*)
[T K]   Capitals in rectangle

KETTEL, THOMAS   *Charlestown, Mass.*   w. 1784
[T. K]   (?)   Capitals with pellet between

KIDNEY, CANN & JOHNSON   *New York, N. Y.*   w. 1850

KIERSTEAD, CORNELIUS   *New York, N. Y.*   1674–1753
                         New Haven, Conn.

[CK]   Crude capitals in rectangle

[CK]   (?)   Crude capitals, lozenge and two pellets
                            below, in shield

[71]

KIMBALL, J.   c. 1785
   [*mark*]   Name in rectangle

KIND, JANE   *Boston, Mass.*   1624–1710

KING, JOSEPH   *Middletown, Conn.*   1770–1807

KINGSTON, JOHN   *New York, N. Y.*   f. 1775

KINNEY, THOMAS   *Norwich, Conn.*   c. 1825
                      (See Thomas Kenney)
   [T K]   Capitals in rectangle

KIP, BENJAMIN   *New York, N. Y.*   f. 1702

KIPPEN, GEORGE   *Middletown, Conn.* b. 1790, w. 1825
                      Bridgeport, Conn.

   [G·KIPPEN]   Roman capitals in rectangle

KIRK, SAMUEL   *Baltimore, Md.*   1793–1872

   [S·KIRK]   Roman capitals in scalloped rectangle

   [S·KIRK]   Roman capitals in rectangle

   [S.K] [11/12]   Roman capitals in rectangle

KIRK, SAMUEL & SON   *Baltimore, Md.*   w. 1846

KIRK & SMITH   *Baltimore, Md.*   w. 1818

KIRTLAND, JOSEPH P.   *Middletown, Conn.* b. 1770, w. 1796

KLINE, B. & CO.   *Philadelphia, Pa.*   w. 1837

KNEELAND, JOSEPH   *Boston, Mass.*   1698–1760

   [I:Kneeland]   Script with Roman capital initials,
                     two pellets between, in cartouche

KRIDER, PETER L.   *Philadelphia, Pa.*   w. 1850
   [P.L.K.]   Capitals

KRIDER & BIDDLE   *Philadelphia, Pa.*

   (K/B)   With pseudo hall-marks

[72]

KUCHER, JACOB — *Philadelphia, Pa.* — w. 1811

[I·KUCHER] Capitals in rectangle

L

LADD, H. H. — c. 1800

LAFORME, F. J. — *Boston, Mass.* — w. 1835

LAFORME, VINCENT — *Boston, Mass.* — w. 1850

V.LAFORME Roman capitals incised

LAKEMAN, E. K. — *Salem, Mass.* — c. 1830

[E.K.LAKEMAN] Small shaded Roman letters in rectangle

LAMAR, MATHIAS — *Philadelphia, Pa.* — w. 1796

[ML] (?) Roman capital monogram in rectangle

LAMB, ANTHONY — *New York, N. Y.* — w. 1760

LAMB, JOHN — *New York, N. Y.* — w. 1756

LAMSON, J. — c. 1790

[J·LAMSON] Thin large Roman capitals in rectangle

[J·L] Roman capitals, pellet between, in cartouche

LANE, AARON — *Elizabethtown, N. J.* — w. 1780

[A. L.] (?) Capitals in cartouche

LANG, EDWARD — *Salem, Mass.* — 1742–1830

[LANG] Roman capitals in rectangle

[EL] Roman capitals in rectangle

LANG, JEFFREY — *Salem, Mass.* — 1707–1758

(I·LANG) Small shaded Roman capitals in long oval

(LANG) Small shaded Roman capitals in long oval

[73]

LANG, RICHARD	*Salem, Mass.*	1733–1820

R·LANG   Roman capitals in rectangle

LANSING, JOHN G.	*Albany, N. Y.*	w. 1780

IGL   Capitals in half oval

LATHROP, RUFUS	*Norwich, Conn.*	1731–1805
LAWRIE, ROBERT D.	*Philadelphia, Pa.*	w. 1841
LEACH, CHARLES	*Boston, Mass.*	c. 1765–1814

CL   Shaded Roman capitals in scalloped rectangle

LEACH, NATHANIEL	*Boston, Mass.*	D. 1789

(*Brother of Charles*)

LEACH, SAMUEL	*Philadelphia, Pa.*	w. 1741
LEACH & BRADLEY	*Utica, N. Y.*	w. 1832
LEACOCK, JOHN	*Philadelphia, Pa.*	w. 1751

I·LEACOCK   Large shaded Roman capitals in rectangle

I.L   Roman capitals in rectangle

I·L   Small shaded Roman capitals in rectangle

I·L   Capitals, pellet between, with emblem above, in cartouche

LEDDEL, JOSEPH J.	*New York, N. Y.*	w. 1752
LEE, THOMAS	*Farmington, Conn.*	1717–1806

(*Partner of Martin Bull*)

LEGARE, DANIEL	*Boston, Mass.*	1688–1724
LEGARE, FRANCIS	*Boston, Mass.*	1636–1711
LENT, JOHN	*Philadelphia, Pa.*	w. 1751

LE RET, PETER	*Baltimore, Md.*	c. 1799
LE ROUX, BARTHOLOMEW	*New York, N.Y.*	d. 1713
LE ROUX, CHARLES	*New York, N. Y.*	f. 1725
[C L]	Capitals in rectangle	
LE ROUX, JOHN	*New York, N. Y.*	f. 1723

[I·L] Roman capitals with pellet between, in rectangle

(IL) Roman capitals in oval

LETELIER, JOHN	*Philadelphia, Pa.*	w. 1770

[I·LT] Shaded Roman capitals with pellet, in rectangle

LEVERETT, KNIGHT	*Boston, Mass.*	1703–1753

(K·Leverett) Script in cartouche

(KL) Capitals in shield

(KL) Capitals in rectangle

LEWIN, GABRIEL	*Baltimore, Md.*	w. 1771

(G L) Roman capitals in rectangle

LEWIS, HARVEY	*Philadelphia, Pa.*	w. 1819

[H·LEWIS] Capitals in rectangle

LEWIS, ISAAC	*Ridgefield, Conn.*	1773–1860

(I·LEWIS) Shaded Roman capitals in rectangle

LEWIS & SMITH	*Philadelphia, Pa.*	w. 1811

(Lewis & Smith) Script in irregular shape

LIBBY, J. G. L.   *Boston, Mass.*   c. 1830

[J.G.L.Libby]   Very small, slightly shaded Roman letters in rectangle

[Libby] [Boston]   Letters in rectangle

LINCOLN, ELIJAH   *Hingham, Mass.*   w. 1818–1833

[E.Lincoln]   Shaded Roman letters in rectangle

LINCOLN & GREEN   c. 1790

[L&G]   Shaded Roman capitals in engrailed rectangle

LINCOLN & REED   *Boston, Mass.*   c. 1848
[*mark*]   Firm name in rectangle

LINTOT   *New York, N. Y.*   w. 1762

LITTLE, WILLIAM   *Newburyport, Mass.*   w. 1775
[W L] (?)   Capitals in rectangle

LITTLETON, T. HODGMAN   after 1800

LOCKWOOD, F.   *New York, N. Y.*   w. 1845

LONG, ROBERT   *Maryland*   b. 1753, w. 1774

LORING, ELIPHALET   *Barnstable, Mass.* b. 1740, m. 1764

[E.Loring]   Large Italic shaded letters in cartouche

LORING, HENRY   *Boston, Mass.*   1773–1818

LORING, JOSEPH   *Hull, Mass.*   1743–1815
                   Boston, Mass.

[J.Loring]   Small shaded Italic letters in cartouche

[J.Loring]   Italics in rectangle

[J.L]   Small shaded Roman capitals in rectangle

[J Loring]   Italics in shaped rectangle

LOSSING, BENSON JOHN   *Poughkeepsie, N. Y.*   1813–1891
        (*The Author and Artist*)

LOUD, ASA   *Hartford, Conn.*   1765–1823

LOW, FRANCIS   *Boston, Mass.*   1806–1855

LOW, JOHN J.   *Salem, Mass.*   c. 1800–1876

LOW, BALL & CO.   *Boston, Mass.*   w. 1840

LOW, JOHN J. & CO.   *Boston, Mass.*   w. 1828

LOWELL & SENTER   *Portland, Me.*   c. 1830
   [*mark*]   Firm name in capitals incised

LOWNES, EDWARD   *Philadelphia, Pa.*   w. 1819
   [E. LOWNES]   In rectangle

LOWNES, JOSEPH   *Philadelphia, Pa.*   w. 1796

   Script letters in irregular shape

LOWNES, J. & J. H.   *Philadelphia, Pa.*   w. 1819

LUSCOMB, JOHN G.   *Boston, Mass.*   w. 1823

LUZERDER, BENJAMIN   *New York, N. Y.*   w. 1796

LYELL, DAVID   *New York, N. Y.*   f. 1699

LYNCH, JOHN   *Baltimore, Md.*   w. 1804

LYNDE, THOMAS   *Worcester, Mass.*   1745–1812

   Shaded Roman capitals in rectangle

LYNG, JOHN   *Philadelphia, Pa.*   w. 1734
   [I. L]   Roman capitals, pellet between, in rectangle

LYNG, JOHN BURT   *New York, N. Y.*   f. 1761

   Capitals in rectangle

   Small Roman capitals, pellet between
             in rectangle

M

MAIN, DAVID   *Stonington, Conn.*   1752–1843

MALRID & CO.   *New York, N. Y.*   w. 1787

MANN, ALEXANDER   *Middletown, Conn.*   b. 1777
    (*Of Brewer & Mann, 1803–1805. See Charles Brewer*)

MANNING, DANIEL   *Boston, Mass.*   w. 1823

MANSFIELD, ELISHA H.   *Norwich, Conn.* b. 1795, w. 1816
    (*Of Coit & Mansfield*)

MANSFIELD, JOHN   *Charlestown, Mass.*   1601–1674

MARBLE, SIMEON   *New Haven, Conn.*   1777–1856
    (*Of Sibley & Marble*)
  [S. MARBLE]   Capitals in rectangle

MARQUAND, FREDERICK   *New York, N. Y.*   c. 1800
  [F. MARQUAND] Roman capitals in rectangle with pseudo
        hall-marks

MARQUAND & CO.   *New York, N. Y.*   c. 1820–1840
  [*mark*]   Firm name with pseudo hall-marks

MARS, S.   c. 1770

[S∷Mars]   Script, six pellets between initials,
        in shaped rectangle

MARSH, B.   *Albany, N. Y.*   c. 1850
  [*mark*]   Name and place in incised capitals with
        pseudo hall-marks

MARSHALL, JOSEPH   *Philadelphia, Pa.*   w. 1819

MARTIN, PETER   *New York, N. Y.*   f. 1756

MARTIN, V.   *Boston, Mass.*   w. 1859

[V.MARTIN]   Small shaded Roman capitals in
        rectangle with PURE COIN, BOSTON,
        and pseudo hall-marks incised

MASI, SERAPHIM	*Washington, D. C.*	w. 1832
MAVERICK, D.	*New York, N. Y.*	

DMN (?) — Shaded Roman capital monogram, in cartouche

MAVERICK, PETER R.	*New York, N. Y.*	1755–1811
McCLINCH, JOHN	*Boston, Mass.*	w. 1760
McCLYMON, J. C.	*New York, N. Y.*	w. 1805
McDOUGALL, WM.	*Meredith, N. H.*	c. 1825
[WM. MCDOUGALL] Capitals in rectangle		
McFARLANE, JOHN	*Boston, Mass.*	d. 1796

J·McFARLANE — Shaded Roman capitals in serrated rectangle

J.McF — Capitals in rectangle

McFEE, JOHN	*Philadelphia, Pa.*	w. 1797
McHARG, ALEXANDER	*Albany, N. Y.*	w. 1849
McMULLIN, JOHN	*Philadelphia, Pa.*	1765–1843

I.McMullin — Roman letters in rectangle

I.M — Capitals in rectangle

McMULLIN & BLACK	*Philadelphia, Pa.*	w. 1811
MEAD, B.	*Massachusetts* (?)	
MEAD, ADRIANCE & Co.	*Ithaca, N. Y.*	w. 1832
MEAD & ADRIANCE	*St. Louis, Mo.*	c. 1820

MEAD ♦ADRIANCE **ST.LOUIS** — Small shaded Roman capitals in rectangle with pseudo hall-marks

MECOM, JOHN	*New York, N. Y.*	d. 1770
MECUM, GEORGE	*Boston, Mass.*	w. 1830

MERICK, J. B.

J.B. Merick   Roman letters in rectangle

MERKLER, JOHN H.   *New York, N. Y.*   w. 1788

MERRIFIELD, THOMAS V. Z. *Albany, N. Y.*   w. 1840
            (*Of Hall, Hewson & Merrifield*)

MERRIMAN, MARCUS   *Cheshire, Conn.*   1762–1850
                        New Haven, Conn.
    (*Of Merriman & Tuttle, 1802; Marcus Merriman & Co.,*
            1802; Merriman & Bradley, 1817)

MM   Crude capitals in rectangle

M (?)   Roman capitals, pellets below, flanked
            with spread eagle, wheat sheaf in ovals

MERRIMAN, MARCUS, JR. *New Haven, Conn.*   w. 1826
            (*Of Bradley and Merriman*)

MERRIMAN, MARCUS & Co. *New Haven, Conn.*   w. 1802

M·M:&CO   Capitals, colons between, in serrated
            rectangle

MERRIMAN, REUBEN   *Litchfield, Conn.*   1783–1866

MERRIMAN, SAMUEL   *New Haven, Conn.*   1769–1805

S.Merriman   Roman letters in rectangle

MERRIMAN, SILAS   *New Haven, Conn.*   1734–1805
            (*Father of Marcus and Samuel*)

MERRIMAN & BRADLEY   *New Haven, Conn.*   w. 1817
            (*M. Merriman, Sr., and Zebul Bradley*)

M&B   Small capitals in rectangle, above,
            a grapevine

MERRIMAN & TUTTLE   *New Haven, Conn.*   w. 1802
            (*M. Merriman, Sr., and B. Tuttle*)

MERROW, NATHAN	*East Hartford, Conn.*	1758–1825
MEYRICK, RICHARD	*Philadelphia, Pa.*	w. 1729
MILES, JOHN	*Philadelphia, Pa.*	w. 1796
MILLAR, J.	*Boston, Mass.*	c. 1825
MILLER, P.		d. 1800
MILLNER, THOMAS	*Boston, Mass.*	c. 1690–c. 1745

 Crude capitals in shaped circle

MILNE, EDMUND	*Philadelphia, Pa.*	w. 1761
MINOTT, SAMUEL	*Boston, Mass.*	1732–1803

Script in rectangle

Script in shaped rectangle

Roman capitals, pellet between, in rectangle

Small script capitals, pellet between, in rectangle

Script capital in square
The first mark above also appears with

Josiah Austin

Wm. Simpkins

MITCHELL, PHINEAS	*Boston, Mass.*	w. 1812
MIX, JAMES	*Albany, N. Y.*	w. 1817
MIX, VISSCHER	*Albany, N. Y.*	w. 1849
MOFFAT, F. W.	*Albany, N. Y.*	w. 1853
MOOD, I.	*Charleston, S. C. (?)*	c. 1800

Roman capitals in two rectangles

MOORE, E. C.	*New York, N. Y.*	w. 1850
MOORE, J. C.	*New York, N. Y.*	w. 1836
MOORE, J. L.	*Philadelphia, Pa.*	c. 1810

[J.L MOORE]   Shaded Roman capitals in rectangle

MOORE, ROBERT	*Maryland*	b. 1737, w. 1774
MOORE & BROWN	*New York, N. Y.*	w. 1833
MOORE & FERGUSON		c. 1800
MORGAN		c. 1800

[*mark*]   Surname incised

MORRIS, JAMES	*Maryland*	b. 1754, w. 1775
MORRIS, JOHN	*New York, N. Y.*	w. 1796
MORRIS, SYLVESTER	*New York, N. Y.*	f. 1759
MORSE, DAVID	*Boston, Mass.*	D. 1798
MORSE, HAZEN	*Boston, Mass.*	w. 1813
MORSE, MOSES	*Boston, Mass.*	w. 1813

[M.MORSE]   Shaded Roman capitals in rectangle

MORSE, NATHANIEL   *Boston, Mass.*   c. 1685–1748

   Roman capitals, crowned, flower (?) below in shaped shield (used in 1711)

   Roman capitals, crowned pellet between, bird below in shield (used in 1739)

[NM]   Sloping capitals in a rectangle

MORSE, STEPHEN   *Newbury, Mass.* b. 1743, w. 1796
Boston, Mass.

SILVERSMITHS AND THEIR MARKS

MOSELEY, DAVID   *Boston, Mass.*   1753–1812

`DMoseley` Italics with shaded Roman initials in rectangle

`DM` Shaded Roman capitals in rectangle

MOSS, ISAAC NICHOLS   *Derby, Conn.*   1760–1840

MOTT, JOHN   *New York, N. Y.*   w. 1789

`J.MOTT` Roman capitals in oval

MOTT, JOHN & WM.   *New York, N. Y.*   w. 1789

MOULINAR, JOHN   *New York, N. Y.*   f. 1744

`I.M` Roman capitals with or without

`IM`   pellet in rectangle

MOULTON, ABEL   *Newburyport, Mass.*   b. 1784
(Brother of Wm. Moulton 4th, b. in 1772)

`A·MOULTON` Shaded Roman capitals in rectangle

MOULTON, EBENEZER   *Boston, Mass.*   b. 1768, D. 1796
(Brother of Wm. Moulton 4th, b. 1772)

MOULTON, EDWARD   *Newburyport, Mass.*   1846–1907
*(Brother of Wm. Moulton 5th, and son of Joseph 3d, with
whom he was associated in business)*
His name does not appear on silver

MOULTON, ENOCH   *Portland, Me.*   b. 1780
(Brother of Wm. Moulton 4th, b. 1772)

`E.MOULTON` Capitals in serrated rectangle

MOULTON, E. S.   c. 1780

`E.S.MOULTON` Roman capitals in serrated rectangle

[83]

SILVERSMITHS AND THEIR MARKS

MOULTON, JOSEPH, 1ST   *Newburyport, Mass.*   1680–1756

[J·M]   Roman capitals, pellet between, in scalloped rectangle

MOULTON, JOSEPH, 2D   *Newburyport, Mass.* c. 1740–1818

[I·MOULTON]   Roman capitals in rectangle

[JM]   Small, script capitals, cross between, in rectangle

[JM]   Script capitals in oval

[IM]   Capitals in rectangle

MOULTON, JOSEPH, 3D   *Newburyport, Mass.*   1814–1903

[J.MOULTON.]   Shaded Roman capitals in rectangle

J.MOULTON   Very small, slightly shaded Roman capitals incised

MOULTON, WILLIAM, 1ST   b. 1602, e. 1638
(*Probably a silversmith as all his descendants were*)

MOULTON, WILLIAM, 2D   *Newburyport, Mass.*   b. 1640
(*Son of William 1st*)

MOULTON, WILLIAM, 3D   *Newburyport, Mass.*   b. 1710
(*Son of Joseph 1st, b. 1680*)

MOULTON, WILLIAM, 4TH   *Newburyport, Mass.*   1720–1793
Marietta, O.
(*Brother of Joseph 2d and son of William 3d*)

MOULTON, WILLIAM, 5TH   *Newburyport, Mass.*   1772–1861
(*Son of Joseph 2d*)

[W·MOULTON]   Shaded Roman capitals in rectangle

[MOULTON]   Shaded Roman capitals in rectangle

MOULTON   Shaded Roman capitals incised

MOULTON, WILLIAM, 6TH   *Newburyport, Mass.*   b. 1851
(*Son of Joseph 3d; of firm of Moulton & Lunt*)

[84]

MOULTON & BRADBURY   *Newburyport, Mass.*   c. 1830

[MOULTON] [B]   Small shaded Roman capitals in rectangle with B in square and two pseudo hall-marks

MOULTON & LUNT   *Newburyport*   late XIX Century
(*Wm. Moulton 6th*)

MULFORD & WENDELL   *Albany, N. Y.*   w. 1842

MUMFORD, HENRY G.   *Providence, R. I.*   w. 1813
(*Partner of Jabez Gorham*)

MUNROE, C. A.

MUNROE, D.
[D. MUNROE]   Capitals in serrated rectangle

MUNROE, JOHN   *Barnstable, Mass.*   1784–1879

[J·MUNROE]   Small shaded Roman capitals in serrated rectangle

MUNSON, AMOS   *New Haven, Conn.*   1753–1785

MUNSON, CORNELIUS   *Wallingford, Conn.*   b. 1742

MURRAY, JOHN   *New York, N. Y.*   w. 1776

MUSGRAVE & JAMES   *Philadelphia, Pa.*   w. 1797–1811

[Musgrave]   Small Italics in shaped rectangle

MYER (or MEYER), GOTTLIEB   *Norfolk, Va.*

MYERS, JOHN   *Philadelphia, Pa.*   w. 1796

[I·MYERS]   Shaded Roman capitals, initials larger, in rectangle

MYERS, MYER   *New York, N. Y.* f. 1746 w. 1790

[Myers]   Shaded Italics in rectangle

[Myers]   Shaded script in cartouche

[85]

Small shaded script capitals in oval

Small crude monogram in cartouche

MYGATT, COMFORT STARR   *Danbury, Conn.*   1763–1823
            (Son of Eli, brother of David)

MYGATT, DAVID   *Danbury, Conn.*   1777–1822
        (Son of Eli, brother and partner of C. S.)

Thin crude slightly shaded letters in rectangle with very fine serrations

MYGATT, ELI   *Danbury, Conn.*   1742–1807
    *(Father of D. and C. S., partner of D. N. Carrington and
                    W. Taylor, 1793)*

N

NEUILL (or NEVILL), RICHARD   *Boston, Mass.*   n. a. f. 1674

NEWBURY, EDWIN C.   *Mansfield, Conn.*   w. 1828
                        Brooklyn, Conn.

NEWHALL, DUDLEY   *Salem, Mass.*   c. 1730
NEWKIRKE, JOSEPH   *New York, N. Y.*   w. 1716

Roman capitals, pellet between, in oval

NEWMAN, TIMOTHY H.   *Groton, Mass.*   1778–1812

Fine script in rectangle

NICHOLS   *Albany, N. Y. (?)*   c. 1840
  [*mark*]   Name incised with pseudo hall-marks

NICHOLS, BASSETT   *Providence, R. I.*   c. 1815

NICHOLS, WILLIAM S.   *Newport, R. I.*   1785–1871
  [NICHOLS] (?)   In long octagon

NICKERSON, BATY   *Harwich, Mass.*   c. 1825

[86]

SILVERSMITHS AND THEIR MARKS

NORCROSS, NEHEMIAH *Boston, Mass.* 1765–1804
[N N] (?) Capitals in cartouche

NORMAN, JOHN *Philadelphia, Pa.* 1748–1817
 Boston, Mass.

NORRIS, GEORGE *Philadelphia, Pa.* b. 1752, w. 1775

NORTH, W. B. *New Britain, Conn.* w. 1831

NORTH, W. B. & Co. c. 1820
[*mark*] Firm name in capitals in rectangle

NORTHEE, DAVID I. *Salem, Mass.* d. 1778

[D·I·NORTHEE] Shaded Roman capitals in rectangle

[DN] Shaded crude capitals in rectangle

NORTHEY, ABIJAH *Salem, Mass.* d. 1817

[AN] (?) Crude capitals in rectangle

NORTON, ANDREW *Goshen, Conn.* 1765–1838

NORTON, BENJAMIN *Boston, Mass.* w. 1810

NORTON, C. after 1800

NORTON, SAMUEL *Hingham, Mass.* c. 1790
 (*Apprentice of L. Bailey*)

NORTON, THOMAS *Farmington, Conn.* 1773–1834
 Albion, N. Y.

[TN] Shaded Roman capitals in rectangle

NOXON

[NOXON] Roman capitals in rectangle

NOYES, JOHN *Boston, Mass.* 1674–1749

[IN] Crude capitals, ecclesiastical cross
 below in shield

[IN] Roman capitals in oval

[87]

SILVERSMITHS AND THEIR MARKS

NOYES, SAMUEL   *Norwich, Conn.*   1747–1781

NUTTALL, JOSEPH   *Maryland*   b. 1738, w. 1774

O

OAKES, FREDERICK   *Hartford, Conn.*   D. 1825
(*See Oakes & Spencer*)

OAKES   Shaded Roman capitals in partly serrated oval

OAKES & SPENCER   *Hartford, Conn.*   w. 1814
(*See Jas. Spencer*)

[O&S]   Capitals in rectangle with pseudo hall-marks

OGIER, JOHN   *Baltimore, Md.*   w. 1799

OLIVER, ANDREW   *Boston, Mass.*   b. c. 1722

[A·OLIVER]   Shaded Roman capitals in rectangle

OLIVER, PETER   *Boston, Mass.*   1682–1712

PO   Large Roman capitals in heart

OLIVIER, PETER   *Philadelphia, Pa.*   w. 1797

OLMSTEAD, NATHANIEL   *New Haven, Conn.*   1785–1860
Farmington, Conn.
(*Of N. Olmstead & Sons, 1847*)

ONCLEBAGH, GARRETT   *New York, N. Y.*   f. 1698

B G O   Crude capitals in trefoil

ONDERDONK, N. & D.   *New York, N. Y. (?)*
[N & D O]   In capitals

O'NEIL, CHARLES   *New Haven, Conn.*   w. 1823
(*With Merriman & Bradley*)

OSGOOD, JOHN   *Haverhill, Mass.*   w. 1795–1817
New Hampshire

J:OSGOOD   Capitals in rectangle

OTIS, JONATHAN   *Newport, R. I.*   1723–1791
Middletown, Conn.

J.Otis   Large script in flat oval

Otis   Small crude letters in flat oval

OTIS   Large crude capitals in rectangle

I·O   Roman capitals, pellet between, in oval

OVERIN, RICHARD   *New York, N. Y.*   f. 1702
OWEN, J.

P

PADDY, SAMUEL   *Boston, Mass.*   b. 1659

PALMER & BATCHELDER   after 1800

PANGBORN & BRINSMAID   *Burlington, Vt.*   c. 1833

P&B   Incised

PARISIEN, DAVID   *New York, N. Y.*   w. 1789–1817
(*Son of Otto*)

PARISIEN, OTTO   *New York, N. Y.*   f. 1769

PARISIEN, O. & SON   *New York, N. Y.*   w. 1789–1817
(*See David Parisien*)

OPDP   Roman capitals in rectangle

PARKER, CHARLES H.   *Salem, Mass.*   1793–1819
Philadelphia, Pa.

SILVERSMITHS AND THEIR MARKS

PARKER, CALEB	*Boston, Mass.*	1731–c. 1770
PARKER, DANIEL	*Boston, Mass.*	1726–1785

(*See Allen, J. & Edwards, J.*)

D:PARKER — Shaded Roman capitals in rectangle

D:P — Shaded Roman capitals, colon between, in rectangle

PARKER, GEORGE	*Baltimore, Md.*	w. 1804
PARKER, ISAAC	*Deerfield, Mass.*	w. 1780

I·PARKER — Shaded Roman capitals in rectangle

PARKER, WILLIAM	*Newport, R. I.*	w. 1777
PARKMAN, JOHN	*Boston, Mass.*	1716–1748
PARMELE, JAMES	*Durham, Conn.*	1763–1828
PARMELE, SAMUEL	*Guilford, Conn.*	1737–1807

S·Parmele — Vertical script in shaped rectangle

SP — Small Roman capitals in rectangle

SP — Small Roman capitals in oval

S·Parmele — Vertical script in rectangle

PARROTT, T.   c. 1760

TPARROTT — Italic capitals in cartouche

PARRY, MARTIN	*Kittery, Me.*	1756–1802
	Portsmouth, N. H.	

PARRY — Small Roman capitals in rectangle

PARSONS   c. 1750

PARSONS — Shaded Roman capitals in rectangle

PATON, A.	*Boston, Mass.*	w. 1850

PATTIT, THOMAS   *New York, N. Y.*   w. 1796
                                (*See Thomas Petit*)

PEABODY, JOHN   *Enfield, Conn.*   w. 1779

`J.PEABODY`   Shaded Roman capitals in rectangle

PEALE, CHARLES WILSON   *Philadelphia, Pa.*   1741–1827
                                (*The artist*)

PEAR, EDWARD   *Boston, Mass.*   w. 1833

`E P`   Roman capitals in cartouche

PEAR & BACALL   *Boston, Mass.*   w. 1850

PEARCE, SAMUEL   *New York, N. Y.*   w. 1783

PEARSON, JOHN   *New York, N. Y.*   w. 1796

PECK, B.   *Connecticut (?)*   c. 1820

`B·PECK`   Roman capitals in rectangle

PECK, TIMOTHY   *Middletown, Conn.*   1765–1818
                                Litchfield, Conn.
PEIRCE   *Boston, Mass.*   c. 1810 (?)

`PEIRCE`   Tiny shaded Roman capitals in rectangle

PELLETRAU, W. S.
  [W. S. PELLETRAU]   Capitals in rectangle

PELLETREAU, ELIAS   *New York, N. Y.*   f. 1736–1810

`EP`   Shaded Roman capitals in rectangle

PEPPER, H. J.   *Philadelphia, Pa.*   c. 1800

`H.I.PEPPER`   Roman capitals in rectangle

`H.J.PEPPER`   Shaded Roman capitals in rectangle

PERKINS, HOUGHTON   *Boston, Mass.*   1735–1778
                                Taunton, Mass.
                                (*Son of Isaac*)

[91]

PERKINS, ISAAC   *Charlestown, Mass.* c. 1707–1737
                       Boston, Mass.

PERKINS, JACOB   *Newburyport, Mass.*   1766–1849
                       Philadelphia, Pa.
*(Partner of Gideon Fairman in Newburyport, partner of
Murray Draper Fairman & Co., Philadelphia)*

PERKINS, JOSEPH,   *South Kingston, R. I.*   b. 1749

PERRAUX, PETER   *Philadelphia, Pa.*   w. 1797
   [P R]   Capitals in rectangle

PERRY, THOMAS   *Westerly, R. I.*

PETERSON, HENRY   *Philadelphia, Pa.*   w. 1783

   [H. P.] (?)   Capitals in a square with pseudo
                       hall-marks

PETIT, THOMAS   *New York, N. Y.*   w. 1796
           (See Thomas Pattit)

PHELPS, JEDEDIAH   *Great Barrington, Mass.*   w. 1781

PHILLIPS, SAMUEL   *Salem, Mass.*   1658–c. 1722
                       Boston, Mass.

   [SP] (?)   Crude capitals in rectangle

PHINNEY & MEAD   c. 1825

   [P&M]   Shaded capitals in rectangle

PIERCE, JOHN   *Boston, Mass.*   c. 1810

PIERPONT, BENJAMIN   *Roxbury, Mass.*   1730–1797

   [B*PIERPONT]   Crude capitals in cartouche

   [B·P]   Small shaded Roman capitals, pellet
                   between, in rectangle

   [PIERPONT]   Capitals in cartouche

   [BP]   Roman capitals in oval

PINCHIN, WILLIAM	*Philadelphia, Pa.*	w. 1784
PINTO, JOSEPH	*New York, N. Y.*	w. 1758
PITKIN, HENRY	*Hartford, Conn.*	b. 1811
PITKIN, HORACE E.	*Hartford, Conn.*	b. 1832
PITKIN, JOB Q.	*Hartford, Conn.*	w. 1780
PITKIN, JOHN O.	*Hartford, Conn.*	1803–1891

PITKIN, J. O. & W.   *Philadelphia, Pa.*   w. 1811–1831
     [J. O. & W. PITKIN]   Capitals in rectangle

PITKIN, WALTER   *Hartford, Conn.*   1808–1885
                  (Brother of J. O.)

PITKIN, WILLIAM L.	*Hartford, Conn.*	b. 1830
PITKINS, JAMES F.	*Hartford, Conn.*	b. 1812

PITMAN, B.   c. 1810
     [B. PITMAN]   In capitals

PITMAN, JOHN K.	*Providence, R. I.*	w. 1805
PITMAN, I.	*Maryland (?)*	c. 1785

Script in cartouche

PITMAN, SAUNDERS   *Providence, R. I.*   1732–1804

Script letters in rectangle

Capitals in serrated rectangle

PITMAN, WILLIAM R.	*New Bedford, Mass.*	c. 1835
PITMAN & DORRANCE	*Providence, R. I.*	w. 1795
PITTS, ABNER	*Berkeley, Mass.*	
PITTS, ALBERT	*Berkeley, Mass.*	
PITTS, RICHARD	*Philadelphia, Pa.*	w. 1741

Script in oval

POINCIGNON, FRANCIS	*Philadelphia, Pa.*	w. 1796
POISSONNIER, F.	*Philadelphia, Pa.*	w. 1797
POLGRAIN, QUOM	*Philadelphia, Pa.*	w. 1797
POLHAMUS, J.	*New York, N. Y.*	w. 1839
POLLARD, WILLIAM	*Boston, Mass.*	1690–1746

(W·P)   Roman capitals in flat oval

PONCET, LEWIS	*Baltimore, Md.*	w. 1804
PONS, THOMAS	*Boston, Mass.*	1757–c. 1817

PONS.   Large Italic capitals in rectangle

[PONS]   Small Roman capitals in rectangle

{PONS}   Large capitals in engrailed rectangle

PONTRAN, ABRAHAM	*New York, N. Y.*	w. 1727

(AP)   Shaded Roman capitals, emblem below
        in heart

POOLE, HENRY	*Maryland*	b. 1754, w. 1775
POOR, NATHANIEL C.	*Boston, Mass.*	1808–1895

PORTER, J. S.
   [I. S. PORTER]   Capitals

PORTER, M. S.   c. 1830
   [M. S. PORTER]   In shaped oval

PORTER, H. & Co.   *Boston, Mass.*   c. 1830
   [*mark*]   Firm name in capitals in rectangle

POST, J.   before 1800

POST, SAMUEL   *Norwich, Conn.*   b. 1736, w. 1783
                      New London, Conn.

POTTER, NILES   *Westerly, R. I.*

POTWINE, JOHN   *Boston, Mass.*   1698–1792
(See Potwine & Whiting)

 Large script in cartouche

 Crude capitals, hyphen between in rectangle

 Shaded Roman capitals, crowned in shaped shield

Crude capitals, pellet between, in small shield

POTWINE & WHITING *Hartford, Conn.* w. 1735
(Probably John Potwine)

POUPARD, JAMES   *Philadelphia, Pa.* w. 1772–1814

PRATT, NATHAN   *Essex, Conn.* 1772–1842

N.PRATT Shaded Roman capitals in rectangle

PRATT, NATHAN, JR. *Essex, Conn.* b. 1802

PRATT, PHINEAS   *Lyme, Conn.* 1747–1813

PRATT, SETH   *Lyme, Conn.* 1741–1802

PRICE, BENJAMIN   *Philadelphia, Pa.* w. 1767

PRICE, JOHN   *Lancaster, Pa.* w. 1764

PRIE, P.   c. 1780

Shaded Roman capitals in cartouche

PRINCE, JOB   *Hull, Mass.* 1680–1703
         Boston, Mass.
         Milford, Conn.

PURSELL, HENRY   *New York, N. Y.* w. 1775

PUTNAM, EDWARD   *Salem, Mass.*   c. 1810

[E.P] (?)   Crude capitals, pellet between, in rectangle

PUTNAM & LOW   *Boston, Mass.*   D. 1822
(*Edw. Putnam and J. J. Low*)

Q

QUINCY, DANIEL   *Braintree, Mass.*   1651–1690

QUINTARD, PETER   *New York, N. Y.*   1699–1762
                          Norwalk, Conn.

[PQ]   Crude capitals in square

[Pq]   Crude capitals in square

R

RAND, JOSEPH   *Medford, Mass.*   1762–1836

RASCH, ANTHONY   *Philadelphia, Pa.*   w. 1815

[ANTY RASCH]   Capitals in rectangle

RASCH, A. & Co.   *Philadelphia, Pa.*   c. 1815
   [mark]   Firm name and city in capitals in rectangles

RASCH & WILLIG   *Philadelphia, Pa.*   w. 1819

RAWORTH, E.   c. 1783
   [E. RAWORTH]   Capitals in rectangle

RAYMOND, JOHN   *Boston, Mass.*   d. 1775

REED, ISAAC   *Stamford, Conn.*   b. 1746

REED, OSMON   *Philadelphia, Pa.*   w. 1843

REED & SLATER   *Nashua, N. H.*

REEDER, ABNER   *Philadelphia, Pa.*   w. 1797

REEVE, G.   c. 1825

G·REEVE — Shaded Roman capitals in scalloped rectangle with pseudo hall-marks

REEVES, ENOS   *Charleston, S. C.*   d. 1807

REEVES — Roman capitals in rectangle

REEVES, STEPHEN   *Burlington, N. J.*   w. 1767–1776
                        New York, N. Y.

REMIER, P. DE

(*See De Remier*)

REVERE, EDWARD   *Boston, Mass.*   1767–1845

REVERE, J. W.   *Boston, Mass.*   D. 1798

REVERE, PAUL, SR., (APPOLOS RIVOIRE)
                        Boston, Mass.   1702–1754

PR — Roman capitals in crowned shield

P.Revere — Italics in rectangle

P.REVERE — Shaded Roman capitals in rectangle

REVERE, PAUL   *Boston, Mass.*   1735–1818
                        (*The patriot*)

·REVERE — Shaded Roman capitals, pellet before, in rectangle

·REVERE — Same as above, but with better made letters

REVERE — Shaded Roman capitals, no pellet, but with the V connected to adjoining letters as well as the first R to the E

REVERE — Same as last but with better made letters and final letters connected

PR — Small crude capitals in rectangle

PR — Capitals incised

PR — Script capitals in rectangle

[97]

REVERE, PAUL, 3D   *Boston, Mass.*   1760–1813

REVERE, THOMAS   *Boston, Mass.*   1765–1817

TR   Crude capitals in rectangle

REVERE & SON   *Boston, Mass.*   D. 1796

REYNOLDS, S. R.   *Boston, Mass.*   after 1800

REYNOLDS, THOMAS   *Philadelphia, Pa.*   w. 1786

RICE   c. 1780

Rice   Small script in flat oval

RICE, JOSEPH T.   *Albany, N. Y.*   w. 1813
  [Joseph T. Rice]   Roman letters
  [Albany]

RICH, JOSEPH   *Philadelphia, Pa.*   w. 1790

RICH, OBADIAH   *Boston, Mass.*   w. 1835

O.RICH
☆ BOSTON ☆   Large shaded Roman capitals incised

RICHARD, S.   *New York, N. Y.*   w. 1828
  [S. RICHARD]   Capitals in rectangle
  [RICHARD]   Capitals in rectangle

RICHARDS, SAMUEL   *Philadelphia, Pa.*   D. 1796

S.RICHARDS   Capitals in rectangle

SRichards   Script in shaped rectangle

RICHARDS, T.   after 1800

T.RICHARDS   Shaded Roman capitals in rectangle

RICHARDS & WILLIAMSON   *Philadelphia, Pa.*   w. 1797

RICHARDSON, FRANCIS   *Philadelphia, Pa.*   f. 1718

SILVERSMITHS AND THEIR MARKS

RICHARDSON, JOSEPH   *Philadelphia, Pa.* w. 1730, d. 1770

(IR)   Capitals in oval

[IR]   Capitals in rectangle

[IR]   Capitals in square

(JR)   Capitals in square or in oval

RICHARDSON, JOSEPH   *Philadelphia, Pa.*   w. 1796

RICHARDSON, THOMAS   *New York, N. Y.*   w. 1769

RICHMOND, G. & A.   *Providence, R. I.*   c. 1815

RIDGWAY, JAMES   *Boston, Mass.*   D. 1789
                       Groton, Mass.   D. 1793

RIDGWAY, JOHN   *Boston, Mass.*   1780–1851

[J:RIDGWAY]   Roman capitals in rectangle

RIDGWAY, JOHN, JR.   *Boston, Mass.*   1813–1869

RIDOUT, GEORGE   *London, England*
                     New York, N. Y.   f. 1745

[GR]   Capitals in a square

RIGGS   *Philadelphia, Pa.*   d. 1819

[Riggs]   Small unshaded Italics in cartouche

RIKER, P.   *New York, N. Y.*   w. 1801
[P. RIKER]   Roman capitals

RIKER & ALEXANDER   *New York, N. Y.*   w. 1798

RITTER, MICHAEL   *New York, N. Y.*   w. 1786

ROATH, ROSWELL WALSTON   *Norwich, Conn.*   b. 1805

ROBBS   *New York, N. Y.*   w. 1788

ROBERT, CHRISTOPHER   *New York, N. Y.*   f. 1731

(C R) (?)   Capitals in circle

[99]

ROBERTS, FREDERICK	*Boston, Mass.*	w. 1770
ROBERTS, MICHAEL	*New York, N. Y.*	w. 1786
ROBERTS, S. & E.		c. 1830
ROBERTS, THOMAS	*Philadelphia, Pa.*	b. 1744, w. 1774
ROBINSON, E.		c. 1780

| E.ROBINSON | Capitals in serrated rectangle |

ROBINSON & HARWOOD	*Philadelphia, Pa.*	w. 1819
ROCKWELL	*Bridgeport, Conn. (?)*	c. 1839

| ROCKWELL | Capitals in rectangle |

ROCKWELL, THOMAS	*Norwalk, Conn.*	d. 1795
ROE, W.	*Kingston, N. Y.*	w. 1803

| W·ROE | Shaded Roman capitals in rectangle with indented ends |

ROGERS, AUGUSTUS	*Boston, Mass.*	w. 1840
ROGERS, DANIEL	*Newport, R. I.*	1753–1792

| D·ROGERS | Roman capitals in rectangle |
| DR | Crude capitals in rectangle |

ROGERS, JOSEPH	*Newport, R. I.*	d. 1825
	Hartford, Conn.	

I R	*(Brother of Daniel, partner of J. Tanner)*
	Capitals in rectangle
JR	Capitals in square

ROGERS, WILLIAM	*Hartford, Conn.*	w. 1825

| Wᵐ ROGERS | Capitals in rectangle |

ROGERS & WENDT	*Boston, Mass.*	w. 1850
ROLLINSON, WILLIAM	*New York, N. Y.*	1762–1842

SILVERSMITHS AND THEIR MARKS

ROMNEY, JOHN   *New York, N. Y.*   f. 1770

ROOSEVELT, NICHOLAS   *New York, N. Y.* f. 1735, w. 1763

    Roman block capitals; N, pellet, R. V.
                        in monogram in oval

    Roman block capitals in monogram in wedge

ROSHORE, JOHN   *New York, N. Y.*   w. 1796

ROUSE, MICHAEL   *Boston, Mass.*   b. 1687, w. 1711

ROUSE, WILLIAM   *Boston, Mass.*   1639–1704

    Shaded Roman capitals, pellet between
                        and below, two above with star in
                        shaped shield

    Crude capitals, fleur-de-lys above and
                        below in circle

ROYALSTON, JOHN   *Boston, Mass.*   w. 1723

  (?)   Roman capitals crowned in shaped shield

[IR] (?)   Roman capitals in rectangle

RULE   *Massachusetts (?)*   c. 1780

[Rule]   Very crude letters in rectangle with
          upper and lower sides scalloped

RUSSEL, JOHN H.   *New York, N. Y.*   w. 1796

RUSSELL, DANIEL   *Newport, R. I.*   c. 1750

[DR]   Roman capitals in a bell

RUSSELL, ELEAZER   *Boston, Mass.*   1663–1691
                      (*Uncle of Moody Russell*)

RUSSELL, GEORGE   *Philadelphia, Pa.*   w. 1831

RUSSELL, JONATHAN   *Ashford, Conn.*   b. 1770, w. 1804

RUSSELL, MOODY   *Barnstable, Mass.*   1694–1761

[MR]   Small Roman capitals in rectangle

[MR]   Large Roman capitals in shaped shield

RYERSON, L.   c. 1800

[*L·Ryerson*]   Script in cartouche

S

SACHEVERELL, JOHN   *Philadelphia, Pa.*   w. 1732

SACKETT & WILLARD   *Providence, R. I.*   c. 1815

SADD, HERVEY   *New Hartford, Conn.*   1776–1840

[H.SADD]   Roman capitals in rectangle

SADTLER, PHILIP   *Baltimore, Md.*   w. 1824

[P.Sadtler]   Roman letters in rectangle

SAINT MARTIN, ANTHONY   *Philadelphia, Pa.*   w. 1796

SALISBURY, H.   c. 1830
[H. SALISBURY] Capitals in rectangle

SALISBURY & CO.   *New York, N. Y.*   c. 1835
[*mark*]   Name in rectangle

SANBORN, A.   *Lowell, Mass.*   w. 1850
[*mark*]   Name in scroll with city in rectangle

SANDERSON, BENJAMIN   *Boston, Mass.*   1649–1678
               (*Son of Robert Sanderson*)

[BS]   Large crude capitals in rectangle

SANDERSON, JOSEPH   1642–1667

SANDERSON, ROBERT   *Boston, Mass.*   1608–1693
           (See Hull & Sanderson)

        Crude capitals, rose above in outline

        Crude capitals, sun above in outline

        Crude capitals, sun in splendor above

SANDERSON, ROBERT, JR.   *Watertown, Mass.*   1652–1714

SANFORD, F. S.   *Nantucket, Mass.*   w. 1830

SANFORD, ISAAC   *Hartford, Conn.*   w. 1793
          (Of Beach & Sanford)

SARDO, MICHAEL   *Baltimore, Md.*   w. 1817

SARGEANT, E.   *Mansfield, Conn.*   1761–1843
                Hartford, Conn.
[E. SARGEANT] Capitals in rectangles
[HARTFORD]

SARGEANT, ENSIGN   *Boston, Mass.*   w. 1823

SARGEANT, JACOB   *Mansfield, Conn.*   1761–1843
                Hartford, Conn.
      (At one time worked with Joseph Church)
[J. SARGEANT] Capitals in rectangles
[HARTFORD]

SARGEANT, T.   *Connecticut*   c. 1810
[T. SARGEANT] Capitals in rectangle

SAVAGE, EDWARD   *Philadelphia, Pa.*   1761–1817
                New York, N. Y.

SAVAGE, THOMAS   *Boston, Mass.*   1664–1749

Crude capitals, star below, in heart

SAWIN, SILAS   *Boston, Mass.*   w. 1823

Small crude letters in flat oval

SAWYER, H. L.   *New York, N. Y.*   c. 1840
                    (*Of Coe & Upton*)

Roman capitals in rectangle

SAYRE, JOEL   *Southampton, L. I.*   1778–1818
                   New York, N. Y.

Shaded Roman capitals in rectangle

Shaded script in shaped rectangle

SCHAATS, BARTHOLOMEW   *New York, N. Y.*   1670–1758

Small crude capitals, fleur-de-lys below
       in heart

SCHANCK, J.   *New York, N. Y.*   w. 1796

Small shaded Roman capitals in
       rectangle with spread eagle and
       false date letter

Small shaded Roman capitals in
       rectangle

SCOFIELD, SOLOMON   *Albany, N. Y.*   w. 1815

SCOTT, JOHN B.   c. 1850
    [*mark*]   Name incised with pseudo hall-marks

SEAL, WILLIAM   *Philadelphia, Pa.*   w. 1819

SEELY   late
    [*mark*]   Name incised with pseudo hall-marks

SILVERSMITHS AND THEIR MARKS

SEXNINE, SIMON   *New York, N. Y.*   w. 1722

SS (?)   Crude capitals in square

SHARP, W. & G.   *Philadelphia, Pa.*   w. 1850

SHAW, JOHN A.   *Newport, R. I.*   w. 1802

I·A·SHAW   Crude capitals in scalloped rectangle

SHEETS   *Henrico, Va.*   w. 1697

SHEPHERD, ROBERT   *Albany, N. Y.*   c. 1800

SHEPHERD   Unshaded Roman capitals incised

SHEPHERD & BOYD   *Albany, N. Y.*   w. 1810

SHEPHERD&BOYD   Roman capitals in rectangle

S&B   Roman capitals in rectangle

SHEPPER, JOHN D.   *Philadelphia, Pa.*   w. 1819

SHERMAN, JAMES   *Boston, Mass.*   c. 1770

SHETHAR, SAMUEL   *Litchfield, Conn.*   w. 1801–1806
                          New Haven, Conn.
(*Shethar & Thomson [Isaac], Shethar & Gorham [Richard]*)

SHIELDS, THOMAS   *Philadelphia, Pa.*   w. 1765

T S (?)   Roman capitals in rectangle

SHIPMAN, NATHANIEL   *Norwich, Conn.*   1764–1853

NS   Shaded Roman capitals in rectangle

SHOEMAKER, JOSEPH   *Philadelphia, Pa.*   w. 1796
[J. SHOEMAKER]   Roman capitals

SHREVE, BENJAMIN   *Salem, Mass.*   1813–1896
                        Boston, Mass.

SHROPSHIRE, ROBT.   *Maryland*   b. 1748, w. 1774

SILVERSMITHS AND THEIR MARKS

SIBLEY, CLARK   *New Haven, Conn.*   1778–1808

SIBLEY & MARBLE   *New Haven, Conn.* w. 1801–1806
(*See Clark Sibley and Simeon Marble*)

SILLIMAN, HEZEKIAH   *New Haven, Conn.*   b. 1738
(*Of Cutler, Silliman, Ward & Co., 1767*)

SIMES, WILLIAM   *Portsmouth, N. H.*   1773–1824
(*Apprentice of Martin Parry*)

| W·SIMES | Large shaded Roman capitals in rectangle |

| W·S | Shaded Roman capitals, pellet between in rectangle |

SIMMONDS, ANDREW   *Philadelphia, Pa.*   w. 1796

SIMMONS, ANTHONY   *Philadelphia, Pa.*   w. 1797

| A.S. | Roman capitals, pellet between and after, in oval |

| A·SIMMONS | Small shaded Roman capitals in rectangle |

SIMMONS, J.   *Philadelphia, Pa.*   c. 1810

| J.Simmons | Script in rectangle |

SIMMONS, J. & A.   *Philadelphia, Pa.*   c. 1810
(*J. & Anthony*)

| J.&A.S | Roman capitals in rectangle |

SIMMONS, S.   *Philadelphia, Pa.*   c. 1797
(*See Alexander & Simmons*)
[S. SIMMONS]   Capitals

SIMPKINS, THOMAS BARTON *Boston, Mass.*   1728–1804
[T. B. Simpkins]   Roman letters

SIMPKINS, WILLIAM	*Boston, Mass.*	1704–1780

W.SIMPKINS   Crude capitals in cartouche

Simpkins   Crude letters, small, in rectangle

W·SIMPKINS   Large shaded Roman capitals in rectangle

W.Simpkins   Script in rectangle

W.S   Capitals in rectangle, pellet between

WS   Capitals in rectangle, no pellet between

SIMPSON & BECKEL	*Albany, N. Y.*	w. 1849
SKAATS, BARTHOLOMEW	*Freeman, N. Y.*	f. 1784
SKATES, JOHN	*Boston, Mass.*	w. 1668–1680
SKERRET, JOSEPH	*Philadelphia, Pa.*	w. 1797
SKERRY, GEORGE W.	*Boston, Mass.*	w. 1837
SKINNER, ABRAHAM	*New York, N. Y.*	f. 1756

Skinner   Crude letters in rectangle

SKINNER, ELIZER	*Hartford, Conn.*	d. 1858
SKINNER, THOMAS		1712–1761

TS   Crude capitals in a rectangle

SLIDEL, JOSHUA	*New York, N. Y.*	f. 1765
SMITH, EBENEZER	*Brookfield, Conn.*	c. 1780
SMITH, DAVID	*Virginia*	b. 1751, w. 1774
SMITH, JAMES	*New York, N. Y.*	w. 1797
SMITH, JOHN & THOMAS	*Baltimore, Md.*	w. 1817

SMITH, JOSEPH	*Boston, Mass.*	d. 1789

I·SMITH — Large shaded Roman capitals in rectangle

I·S (?) — Roman capitals, pellet between, in rectangle

SMITH, WILLIAM	*New York, N. Y.*	w. 1770
SMITHER, JAMES	*Philadelphia, Pa.*	w. 1768–1777
	New York, N. Y.	
SNOW, J.		c. 1770

J:SNOW — Shaded Roman capitals in rectangle

SOMERBY, ROBERT	*Boston, Mass.*	1794–1821
SOUMAINE, SAMUEL	*Philadelphia, Pa.*	w. 1765

S S (?) — Small Roman capitals in rectangle

(*This mark is smaller than the one attributed to Simeon Soumaine*)

SOUMAINE, SIMEON	*New York, N. Y.*	w. 1719

SS — Large thin crude capitals in square

SS — Large thin crude capitals in circle

SPENCER, GEORGE	*Essex, Conn.*	1787–1878
SPENCER, JAMES	*Hartford, Conn.*	w. 1793
SQUIRE & BROS.	*New York, N. Y.*	w. 1846
STACY, P.	*Boston, Mass.*	w. 1819

P.STACY — Shaded Roman capitals in rectangle

STALL, JOSEPH	*Baltimore, Md.*	w. 1804
STANIFORD, JOHN	*Windham, Conn.*	w. 1790

STANTON, DANIEL   *Stonington, Conn.*   1755–1781

[D.Stanton]   Roman letters in rectangle

STANTON, ENOCH   *Stonington, Conn.*   1745–1781

STANTON, WILLIAM   w. 1802

STANTON, ZEBULON   *Stonington, Conn.*   1753–1828

[Z S]   Roman capitals in rectangle with emblem

STANWOOD, HENRY B.   *Boston, Mass.*   1818–1869

STANWOOD, JAMES D.   *Boston, Mass.*   w. 1846

STANWOOD & HALSTRICK   *Boston, Mass.*   c. 1850

STAPLES, JOHN J., JR.   *New York, N. Y.*   w. 1788

STARR, JASPER   *New London, Conn.*   1709–1792

STARR, R.   c. 1800

[R·STARR]   Roman capitals in rectangle

STEBBINS, E. & Co.   *New York, N. Y.*   w. 1841

[E.STEBBINS&CO]   Capitals in rectangle

STENSON, W. S.

STEPHENS, GEORGE   *New York, N. Y.*   w. 1790

[G.S]   Shaded Roman capitals in serrated
                        end cartouche

STEVENS & LAKEMAN   *Salem, Mass.*   w. 1825

[STEVENS&LAKEMAN]   Small shaded Roman
                        capitals in rectangle

STICKNEY, JONATHAN   *Newburyport, Mass.*   w. 1770

[I·STICKNEY]   Shaded crude capitals in rectangle
                        sometimes flanked by lions
                        passant in rectangles

[109]

STILES, BENJAMIN   *Woodbury, Conn.*   c. 1825
    (*Of Curtiss Candee & Stiles, see Daniel Curtiss*)

STILLMAN, BARTON   *Westerly, R. I.*   1767–1858

STILLMAN, E.   *Stonington (?), Conn.* c. 1800–1820

[E.Stillman]   Roman letters in rectangle

STILLMAN, PAUL   *Westerly, R. I.*

STILLMAN, WILLIAM   *Hopkinton, R. I.*   1767–1858

STOCKERMAN & PEPPER   *Philadelphia, Pa.*   c. 1840
  [mark]   Firm name in oval

STODDER & FROBISHER   *Boston, Mass.*   w. 1817
  [mark]   Firm name in thin shaded Roman
              capitals in rectangle

STONE, ADAM   *Baltimore, Md.*   w. 1804

STONE & OSBURN   *New York, N. Y.*   w. 1796

STORRS, N.   *Utica, N. Y. (?)*   c. 1800

[N.STORRS]   Large shaded Roman capitals
              in rectangle

STORRS & COOLEY   *Utica, N. Y.*   w. 1832

STOUT, J. D.   c. 1850
  [J. D. STOUT]   In serrated rectangle

STOUTENBURGH, TOBIAS   *New York, N. Y.*   f. 1731
  [T. S.]   Capitals in rectangle

STOWELL, A., JR.   *Charlestown, Mass.*
  [mark]   Name in capitals in rectangle, place in
            small letters in long oval

STRONG, JOHN   *Maryland*   b. 1749, w. 1774

STUART, I. (or J.)   c. 1700

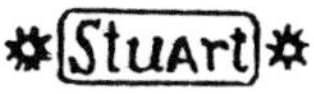

�֍ Stuart ✖   Crude letters in rectangle, flanked by suns incised

IS   Crude shaded capitals in rectangle

STUDLEY, D. F.   c. 1830

D.F. STUDLEY.   Very small shaded Roman capitals in rectangle

SUTHERLAND, GEORGE   *Boston, Mass.*   w. 1810

SUTTON, ROBERT   *New Haven, Conn.*   D. 1825

SWAN, B.   c. 1825

B.SWAN   Capitals in rectangle

SWAN, CALEB   *Charlestown, Mass.*   1754–1816
                Boston, Mass.

SWAN, ROBERT   *Worcester, Mass.*   w. 1775

R SWAN   Capitals in rectangle

SWAN, WILLIAM   *Worcester, Mass.*   1715–1774

WSWAN   Crude capitals in cartouche

Swan   Script in cartouche

WS (?)   Block capitals in cartouche

SYMMES, JOHN   *Boston, Mass.*   w. 1766

SYNG, PHILIP   *Philadelphia, Pa.*   1676–1739

PS   Roman capitals in rectangle

SYNG, PHILIP   *Philadelphia, Pa.*   1703–1789

T

TANGUEY, I.   c. 1825

TANNER, JOHN   *Newport, R. I.*   1713–1785
                 (Partner of Jos. Rogers)

TARBELL, E.   c. 1830
   [mark]   Name in capitals in rectangle

TARGEE, JOHN & PETER   *New York, N. Y.*   D. 1798

   I & PT   Roman capitals in rectangle with
                        pseudo hall marks

   I & P.TARGEE   Shaded Roman capitals in rectangle

TAYLOR, NAJAH   *Danbury, Conn.*   w. 1793
       (Partner of E. Mygatt and D. N. Carrington)

TAYLOR, WILLIAM   *Philadelphia, Pa.*   w. 1772

TAYLOR & LAWRIE   *Philadelphia, Pa.*   w. 1841

TEMPLEMAN, JOHN   *Carolina*   b. 1746, w. 1774

TEN EYCK, J.   *Albany, N. Y.*   c. 1725

   IT   Crude capitals in oval

   IE   Crude capital monogram in square

TEN EYCK, KEONRAET   *New York, N. Y.*   f. 1716
                        Albany, N. Y.

   KE   Crude capital monogram in square

TERRY, GEER   *Enfield, Conn.*   1775–1858
                        Worcester, Mass.

   G.TERRY   Roman capitals in rectangle

   TERRY   Roman capitals in rectangle

SILVERSMITHS AND THEIR MARKS

THAXTER, JOSEPH BLAKE   *Hingham, Mass.*   1791–1863
            (*The last silversmith in Hingham*)

THIBARULT & CO.   *Philadelphia, Pa.*   w. 1797

THOMAS, WALTER   *New York, N. Y.*   f. 1769

THOMSON, ISAAC   *Litchfield, Conn.*   c. 1800
            (*See Shethar & Thomson*)

THOMSON, JAMES   *New York, N. Y.*   w. 1839

THOMSON, PETER   *Boston, Mass.*   w. 1817

THOMSON, WILLIAM   *New York, N. Y.*   w. 1830

[*W ͫ Thomson*]   Script in shaped rectangle

TIEBOUT, CORNELIUS   *New York, N. Y.*   1770–1830
            (*Apprentice of John Burger*)

TILEY, JAMES   *Hartford, Conn.*   1740–1792

[I·TILEY]   Shaded Roman capitals in rectangle

[Tiley]   Shaded Roman letters in rectangle

TINGLEY, SAMUEL   *New York, N. Y.*   w. 1767
                         Philadelphia, Pa.

TISDALE, B. H.   *Newport, R. I.*   c. 1825
    [mark]   Name and place in capitals in rectangles

TITCOMB, FRANCIS   *Newburyport, Mass.*   w. 1813

[F.TITCOMB]   Small shaded Roman capitals in rectangle

TOMPKINS, EDMUND   *Waterbury, Conn.* b. 1757, w. 1779

TOPPAN, BENJ.   *Northampton, Mass.*   c. 1760
            (*Apprentice and son-in-law of Wm. Homes*)

TOWNSEND, S.   c. 1775

[*Townsend*]   Script in rectangle

[S.TOWNSEND]   Shaded Roman capitals in rectangle

[113]

TOWZELL, JOHN   *Salem, Mass.*   c. 1726–1785
[J. Towzell]   Roman letters
[I T]   Roman capitals

TRACY, ERASTUS   *Norwich, Conn.*   1768–1795
(*Brother of Gurdon*)

TRACY, GURDON   *Norwich, Conn.*   1767–1792
New London, Conn.

TREZVANT, DANIEL   *Charleston, S. C.*   w. 1768

TROTT, GEORGE   *Boston, Mass.*   c. 1765

TROTT, JOHN PROCTOR   *New London, Conn.*   1769–1852
(*Son of J.*)

[J·P·TROTT]   Roman capitals in long oval

[J·P·T]   Roman capitals in serrated rectangle

[JPT]   Script capitals in oval

[JPT | & Son]   Roman capitals in divided rectangle

TROTT, JONATHAN   *Boston, Mass.*   1730–1815
New London, Conn.

[J.TROTT]   Roman capitals in cartouche

[I.TROTT]   Roman capitals in rectangle

TROTT, JONATHAN, JR.   *New London, Conn.*   1771–1813

[I.T] (?)   Capitals in rectangle

TROTT, THOMAS   *Boston, Mass.*   c. 1701–1777

[T·T]   Large Roman capitals in rectangle

[T·T] (?)   Small Roman capitals, crowned, in cartouche

[T·T]   Roman capitals, pellet between, crowned, in rectangle

TROTT & BROOKS	*New London, Conn.*	w. 1798
	(J. P. Trott)	
TROTT & CLEVELAND	*New London, Conn.*	w. 1792
	(J. P. Trott & Wm. Cleveland)	

[T⊎C] Capitals in rectangle

TRUAX, HENRY R.	*Albany, N. Y.*	w. 1815
TURNER, JAMES	*Boston, Mass.* w. 1744, d. 1759	
	Philadelphia, Pa.	
	(Well known as an engraver)	

[IT] (?) Roman capitals in shaped shield

[IT] (?) Roman capitals, small in rectangle

TUTHILL, CHRISTOPHER	*Philadelphia, Pa.*	w. 1730
TUTTLE, BETHUEL	*New Haven, Conn.*	1779–1813

(Of Merriman & Tuttle, 1802–1806; M. Merriman & Co., 1806–1813)

TUTTLE, WILLIAM	*New Haven, Conn.*	1800–1849
	Suffield, Conn.	
TYLER, ANDREW	*Boston, Mass.*	1692–1741

[AT] Roman capitals, fleur-de-lys below, in
        heart

[AT] Crude capitals, crowned, emblem below,
        in shaped shield

[AT] Gothic capitals, crowned, in shield with
        rounded base

[A·TYLER] Small Roman capitals, in long oval

[AT] Roman capitals in rectangle

[115]

TYLER, DAVID   *Boston, Mass.*   c. 1760–1804

[DT]   Roman capitals in rectangle

[DT]   Roman capitals in book

TYLER, GEORGE   *Boston, Mass.*   b. 1740, w. 1785
                          (Grandson of Andrew)

[GT]   Roman capitals in rectangle

U

UFFORD & BURDICK   *New Haven, Conn.*   w. 1814
                          (See W. S. Burdick)

UNDERHILL, ANDREW   *New York, N. Y.*   w. 1788

[A·UNDERHILL]   Small shaded Roman capitals
                 in rectangle

[A·U]   Small shaded Roman capitals
                 in oval

UNDERHILL, THOMAS   *New York, N. Y.*   f. 1787
                 Shaded Roman capitals hyphen between,
[T·U]   in rectangle

UNDERHILL & VERNON   *New York, N. Y.*   w. 1786
                 (Thos. Underhill and John Vernon)

[T·U] [I·V]   Shaded Roman capitals in rectangle
                 and in cartouche

V

VAN BERGEN, JOHN   *Albany, N. Y.*   w. 1813

VAN BEUREN, P.   *New York, N. Y.*   w. 1790

[VB]   Shaded Roman capitals in decorated oval

[116]

VAN BEUREN, WM.   *New York, N. Y.*   w. 1797

(W.V.B)   Shaded Roman capitals in cartouche

VANDERHAUL   *Philadelphia, Pa.*   w. 1740

VAN DER SPIEGEL, JACOBUS *New York, N. Y.*

w. 1685, d. c. 1708

(S / I.V)   Crude capitals in trefoil

VAN DER SPIEGEL, JOHANNES   *New York, N. Y.*   1666–1716
(*Brother of Jacobus*)

[IVS]   Shaded Roman capitals in engrailed
rectangle

VAN DYKE, PETER   *New York, N. Y.*   1684–1750

(P·V·D)   Roman capitals, pellets between, in oval

(PVD)   Roman capitals, no pellets between, in oval

[P·V·D]   Roman capitals, pellets between, in rectangle

(V / P·D)   Shaded Roman capitals, pellet between, in trefoil

VAN DYKE, RICHARD   *New York, N. Y.*   w. 1750
(*Son of Peter*)

[RVD]   Roman capitals in rectangle

VAN NESS & WATERMAN   *New York, N. Y.* (?)

[V & W]   Capitals in rectangle

VAN SCHAICK, G.   c. 1840

[G V"Schaick]   Italic letters in rectangle

[117]

VAN VOORHIS, DANIEL   *Philadelphia, Pa.*   w. 1782–1787
                                         New York, N. Y.

D.V.   Roman capitals, pellet between, in
        rectangle with an eagle in lozenge

D.V.V.   Roman capitals, pellets between, in
          rectangle, eagle in lozenge

D.V.VOORHIS   Shaded Roman capitals in rectangle
               with two eagles in lozenges

D.V.V   Roman capitals, pellets between, in
         oval with similar eagles

D♥V   Roman capitals in lozenge, eagle
V   in centre

VAN VOORHIS & COOLY   *New York, N. Y.*   w. 1786

VAN VOORHIS & SON   *New York, N. Y.*   w. 1798

V.V.♥S.   Shaded Roman capitals in rectangle

VEAZIE, JOSEPH   *Providence, R. I.*   c. 1815

VEAZIE, SAMUEL & JOS.   *Providence, R. I.*   c. 1820

VERGEREAU, PETER   *New York, N. Y.*   f. 1721

VERNON, DANIEL   *Newport, R. I.*   b. 1716

VERNON, JOHN   *New York, N. Y.*   w. 1789

I·V   Shaded Roman capitals in cartouche

IV (?)   Shaded Roman capitals in oval with
           sheaf of wheat in rectangle

VERNON, J. & CO.   *New York, N. Y.*   w. 1796

VERNON, NATHANIEL   *Charleston, S. C.*   1777–1843

N.VERNON   Roman capitals in rectangle

NV   Shaded Roman capitals in rectangle

VERNON, SAMUEL   *Newport, R. I.*   1683–1737

 Roman capitals, fleur-de-lys below in heart
    (*There are two sizes in this mark, one
    being quite small for use on little
    objects.*)

VILANT, WILLIAM   *Philadelphia, Pa.*   w. 1725

 Capitals, fleur-de-lys, below, in heart

VINCENT, RICHARD   *Baltimore, Md.*   w. 1799

VINTON, DAVID   *Boston, Mass.*   w. 1792
                 Providence, R. I.

D.V (?)   Roman capitals, pellet below, in
        rectangle

VIRGIN, W. M.   c. 1830
[*mark*]   Name in rectangle

W

WAITE, JOHN   *Kingston, R. I.*

I.WAITE   Capitals in rectangle

[J. WAITE]   Capitals in rectangle

WAITE, JONATHAN   *Wickford, R. I.*   1730–1822

WAITE, W.   c. 1770

W:WAITE   Roman capitals in rectangle

WALCOTT, HENRY D.   *Boston, Mass.*   1797–1830
            (*Of Walcott & Gelston*)

WALCOTT & GELSTON   *Boston, Mass.*   w. 1824

WALKER, GEORGE   *Philadelphia, Pa.*   w. 1796

WALKER, WILLIAM   *Philadelphia, Pa.*   w. 1796
  [W. WALKER]   Capitals in rectangle

WALLACE, WILLIAM F.   *Westerly, R. I.*

WALRAVEN   *Baltimore, Md.*   w. 1796
  [*mark*]   Name in script

WALSH   c. 1780
  [WALSH]   Capitals in rectangle

WALWORTH, DANIEL   *Middletown, Conn.*   1760–1830

WARD   *Philadelphia, Pa.*   w. 1774
           (*Partner of John Norman*)

WARD, AMBROSE   *New Haven, Conn.*   1735–1808
       (*Of Cutler, Silliman, Ward & Co.*)

WARD, BILLIOUS   *Guilford, Conn.*   1729–1777

BW   Crude capitals in rectangle

BW   Crude capitals in oval, engrailed at
                 one end

BW   Crude capitals in oval

WARD, JAMES   *Guilford, Conn.*   1768–1856
    (*See Beach & Ward and Ward & Bartholomew*)
  [J. WARD]   Capitals in rectangle
  [WARD]
  [HARTFORD] } Capitals incised

WARD, JOHN   *Middletown, Conn.*   w. 1805
     (*Of Ward & Hughes. See Edmund Hughes*)

WARD, JOHN   *Philadelphia, Pa.*   w. 1811
  [Ward, 67 Market St.]   Roman letters

WARD, MACOCK   *Wallingford, Conn.*   b. 1705

WARD, RICHARD   *Boston, Mass.*   c. 1815

WARD, SAMUEL L.   *Boston, Mass.*   w. 1834

WARD, TIMOTHY	*Middletown, Conn.*	1742–1768
WARD, WILLIAM	*Wallingford, Conn.*	1678–1767
WARD, WILLIAM	*Guilford, Conn.*	1705–1761

(*Father of Billious and Son of William*)

[W.WARD]   Capitals in rectangle

[W.W.]   Capitals in rectangle

[W.Ward]   Script in rectangle

WARD, WILLIAM	*Litchfield, Conn.*	1736–1826
WARD & BARTHOLOMEW	*Hartford, Conn.*	w. 1804–1809

(*Jas. Ward and Roswell Bartholomew*)

[WARD ♥ BARTHOLOMEW]
[HARTFORD]   Capitals in rectangle

[W ♥ B]
[HARTFORD]   Capitals in rectangle

[WARD ♥ BARTHOL
OMEW.HARTFORD]   Capitals in rectangle

WARD, BARTHOLOMEW & BRAINARD *Hartford, Conn.* w. 1809
(*See previous firm and Chas. Brainard*)

WARD & COX	*Philadelphia, Pa.*	w. 1811
WARD & JONES		late
WARD & RICH	*Boston, Mass.*	w. 1833
WARDIN, DANIEL	*Bridgeport, Conn.*	w. 1811
WARNER, ANDREW E.	*Baltimore, Md.*	w. 1811

[AE WARNER]   Capitals in rectangle

WARNER, ANDREW E., JR. *Baltimore, Md.* w. 1837
[A. E. WARNER]   Capitals in rectangle
(*Probably used his father's mark*)

WARNER, A. E. & T. H. *Baltimore, Md.* w. 1805

WARNER, CALEB   *Salem, Mass.*   1784–1861

[C.Warner]   Roman letters in rectangle

[Pure SilverCoin]   Roman letters in shaped rectangle

WARNER, C. & J.

[C.& J.WARNER]   Capitals in rectangle

WARNER, D.   *Ipswich, Mass. (?)*   c. 1810

[D.WARNER]   Small shaded Roman capitals in
                    scalloped rectangle

WARNER, JOSEPH   *Philadelphia, Pa.*   w. 1811
[J. Warner]   Roman letters in rectangle

WARNER, S.   *Baltimore, Md.*   c. 1812

[SW]   Capitals in rectangle

WARNER, SAMUEL   *Philadelphia, Pa.*   w. 1797

WARNER, T.   late
[T. WARNER]   Capitals in rectangle with pseudo hall-
                    marks

WARNER, THOMAS H.   *Baltimore, Md.*   w. 1814

WATERMAN, GEORGE   *Albany, N. Y.*   w. 1849

WATERS, SAMUEL   *Boston, Mass.*   w. 1804

[S.WATERS]   Roman capitals in rectangle

[S·W]   Shaded Roman capitals in rectangle

(S.W)   (?)   Large shaded Roman capitals, pellet
                    between, in oval

WATSON, EDWARD   *Boston, Mass.*   w. 1821, d. 1839
[E. WATSON]   Capitals in rectangle
[E. Watson]   Letters in rectangle

[122]

WATSON & BROWN   *Boston, Mass. (?)*   c. 1830
  [*mark*]   Firm name in capitals in rectangle

WATTS, J. & W.   *Philadelphia, Pa.*   w. 1841

WAYNES, RICHARD   c. 1750

     Running capitals in cartouche, with
            golden fleece in rectangle

WEBB, BARNABAS   *Boston, Mass.* b. c. 1729, w. 1786
            Thomaston, Me.

(?)   Small crude capitals, in rectangle

WEBB, GEORGE W.   *Baltimore, Md.*   w. 1850

WEBB, JAMES   *Baltimore, Md.*   w. 1817

WEBSTER, H. L.   *Providence, R. I.*   w. 1831–1841
            Boston, Mass.

WEDGE, SIMON   *Baltimore, Md.*   w. 1804

WEEDEN, PELEG   *North Kingston, R. I.*   c. 1803

WELSH, JOHN   *Boston, Mass.*   1730–1812

WELLES, A. & G.   *Boston, Mass.*   c. 1810
  [A. & G. Welles]   Roman letters in rectangle
  [A. & G. W.]   Roman capitals in rectangle

WELLES, ANDREW   *Hebron, Conn.*   1783–1860

WELLES, GEORGE   *Hebron, Conn.*   1784–1827
            Boston, Mass.

    Capitals in rectangle

WELLES & CO.   *Boston, Mass.*   c. 1800
  [WELLES & CO.]   Roman capitals in rectangles

WELLES & GELSTON
  [Welles & Gelston]   Roman letters in rectangle

WELLS, TAIN, & HALL   after 1800
   [L. T. Welles]
   [A. S. Tain]   Roman letters
   [D. G. Hall]

WELLS, WILLIAM   *Hartford, Conn.*   b. 1766, D. 1828

WENDOVER, JOHN   *New York, N. Y.*   1694–1727

J·W   Large crude capitals, pellet between,
               in cartouche

WENDT, J. R. & Co.

WENMAN, BARNARD   *New York, N. Y.*   w. 1786

BWENMAN   Shaded Roman capitals in rectangle

WEST, B.   *Boston, Mass.*   w. 1770

B.WEST   Capitals in rectangle

WEST, CHARLES   *Boston, Mass.*   c. 1830

WESTERVELL, J. L.   *Newburgh, N. Y.*   w. 1852
   [J. L. W.]   With pseudo hall-marks

WESTPHAL, C.   *Philadelphia, Pa.*   w. 1800

C.WESTPHAL   In cartouche

WHARTENBY, JOHN   *Philadelphia, Pa.*   w. 1831

WHARTENBY, THOMAS   *Philadelphia, Pa.*   w. 1811

WHARTENBY, THOMAS & Co.   *Philadelphia, Pa.*   w. 1850

WHEATON, CALEB   *Providence, R. I.*   1784–1827

WHEATON, CALVIN   *Providence, R. I.*   w. 1790

C WHEATON   Capitals in rectangle

WHETCROFT, WILLIAM   *Annapolis, Md.*   w. 1766

WHIPPLE, ARNOLD   *Providence, R. I.*   D. 1825

SILVERSMITHS AND THEIR MARKS

WHITAKER & GREENE   *Providence, R. I.*   c. 1825

WHITE, AMOS   *Haddam Landing, Conn.*   1745–1825
                   Meriden, Conn.

WHITE, E.   before 1760
  [E : WHITE]   Capitals in rectangle
  [E W]   Capitals in rectangle

WHITE, PEREGRINE   *Woodstock, Conn.*   1747–1834
  [P. WHITE] (?) Capitals in rectangle
            (*This mark may be that of Peter*)

WHITE, PETER   *Norwalk, Conn.*   1718–1803

WHITE, THOMAS STURT   *Boston, Mass.*   w. 1734

WHITING, CHARLES   *Norwich, Conn.*   1725–1765

WHITLOCK, THOMAS   *New York, N. Y.*   w. 1796

WHITNEY, M.   *New England (?)*   c. 1823

[M.WHITNEY]   Small unshaded Roman capitals in
               rectangle

WHITON, EBED   *Boston, Mass.*   1802–1879

[E.Whiton.]   Small Roman letters in rectangle and
               in scroll

WHITTEMORE, EDWARD   *Boston, Mass.*   d. 1772

WHITTEMORE, WILLIAM   *Portsmouth, N. H.*   1710–1770

[Whittemore]   Italic letters in rectangle

WHITTLESEY   *Vincennes, Ind.*   w. 1808

WILCKE   c. 1810
  [WILCKE]   Capitals in rectangle with pseudo
              hall-marks

WILLCOX, ALVAN   *Norwich, Conn.*   1783–1865
                      New Haven, Conn.
            (*See Hart & Willcox*)

[125]

WILLCOX, CYPRIAN   *New Haven, Conn.*   1795–1875
     (*Brother of Alvan*)

WILLIAMS, ANDREW
   [ANDREW WILLIAMS]   Capitals

WILLIAMS, DEODAT   *Hartford, Conn.*   w. 1775, d. 1781

WILLIAMS, SAMUEL   *Philadelphia, Pa.*   w. 1796

WILLIAMS, STEPHEN   *Providence, R. I.*   w. 1799

WILLIAMSON, SAMUEL   *Philadelphia, Pa.*   w. 1796

[WILLIAMSON]   Small shaded Roman capitals
     in rectangle

WILLIG, GEORGE   *Philadelphia, Pa.*   w. 1819

WILLIS, STILLMAN   *Boston, Mass.*   w. 1823

WILMOT, SAMUEL, JR.   *New Haven, Conn.*   1777–1846
     (*Of Wilmot & Stillman*)
   [WILMOT]   Capitals in serrated rectangle

WILMOT & STILLMAN   *New Haven, Conn.*   w. 1800
     (*See Samuel Wilmot*)

WILSON, ALBERT   *Troy, N. Y.*   w. 1834

WILSON, GEORGE   *Philadelphia, Pa.*   w. 1819

WILSON, HOSEA   *Baltimore, Md.*   w. 1817
   [H. WILSON]   Roman capitals

WILSON, R. & W.   *Philadelphia, Pa.*   w. 1831

[R & WW]   Roman capitals in rectangle

WILSON, RICHARD   *New York, N. Y.* b. 1758, w. 1774

WILSON, ROBERT   *Philadelphia, Pa.*   w. 1819

WILSON, S. N.   *Connecticut*   c. 1800
   [S. N. WILSON]   Capitals in rectangle

WILSON, WILLIAM	*Philadelphia, Pa.*	w. 1850
WILTBERGER, CHRISTIAN	*Philadelphia, Pa.*	w. 1793

[C. Wiltberger]   Script in irregular shape

WINSLOW, EDWARD	*Boston, Mass.*	1669–1753

[EW]   Shaded Roman capitals, fleur-de-lys below, in shaped shield

[EW]   Shaded Roman capitals in rectangle

(EW)   Shaded Roman capitals in double circles

WISE, W. M.	*Brooklyn, N. Y.*	c. 1800
WISHART, HUGH	*New York, N. Y.*	
		D. 1789 and 1816

[H.WISHART]   Shaded Roman capitals in rectangle

[WISHART]   Shaded Roman capitals in rectangle with and without pseudo hall-marks

WITHERS, JAMES	*Maryland*	b. 1753, w. 1774
WOLCOTT & GELSTON	*Boston, Mass. (?)*	c. 1824

[Wolcott & Gelston]   Shaded Roman letters in rectangle

WOOD, ALFRED	*New England (?)*	c. 1800

[WOOD] (?)   Thin slightly shaded Roman capitals in rectangle with fine serrations

WOOD, BENJ.	*New York, N. Y. (?)* w. 1794–1812

[B. WOOD]   Capitals with pseudo hall-marks

WOOD, J. E.	*New York, N. Y.*	w. 1845

WOOD & HUGHES   *New York, N. Y.*   w. 1845

[W&H]   In rectangle with eagle and head

[W&H diamond]   In diamond with eagle and head

WOODBURY, DIX & HARTWELL   c. 1836
[*mark*]   Firm name in small capitals in rectangle

WOODCOCK, BANCROFT   *Wilmington, Del.* c. 1735–c. 1820

WOODS, FREEMAN   *New York, N. Y.*   w. 1790–1793

[Woods]   Shaded script in cartouche

WOODWARD, ANTIPAS   *Middletown, Conn.* b. 1763, w. 1791

[Woodward]   Roman letters with decorative d's in rectangle

[AW]   Capitals in rectangle

WOODWARD, ELI   *Hartford, Conn.*   w. 1812

WOODWARD & GROSJEAN   *Boston, Mass.*   w. 1847

WOOL, JEREMIAH WARD   *New York, N. Y.*   f. 1791

WRIGGINS, THOMAS   *Philadelphia, Pa.*   w. 1841

WRIGHT, ALEXANDER   *Maryland*   b. 1748, w. 1775

WRIGHT, W.

[W.Wright]   Semi-script letters in oval

WYATT, JOSEPH   *Philadelphia, Pa.*   w. 1797

WYER, ELEAZER   *Charlestown, Mass.*   1752–1800

WYER, ELEAZER, JR.   *Portland, Me.*   1786–1848

[E.WYER]   Large capitals in rectangle

[E.WYER]   Capitals in serrated rectangle

WYER & FARLEY   c. 1830
[mark]   Firm name in rectangle, flanked by
                  eagle in oval

WYNKOOP, BENJAMIN   *New York, N. Y.*

                                            bap. 1675 w. 1740

              Crude capitals, pellet between, in heart

  Capitals in long oval

WYNKOOP, CORNELIUS   *New York, N. Y.* b. 1701, f. 1727
                        (*Son of Benjamin*)

              Crude capitals in heart

Y

YATES, S.   c. 1825

[S.YATES]   Thin shaded Roman capitals in serrated
                  rectangle

YEOMANS, ELIJAH   *Hartford, Conn.*   1738–1794

YETTONS, RANDAL   *Philadelphia, Pa.*   w. 1739

YOUNG, EBENEZER   *Hebron, Conn.*   w. 1778

YOUNG, LEVI   *Bridgeport, Conn.*   w. 1827

YOUNG, WILLIAM   *Philadelphia, Pa.*   w. 1761

GLOSSARY

GLOSSARY

A

ALLOY — A baser metal mixed with silver in various proportions to give it the required degree of hardness for working and wear, pure copper being the usual ingredient. See *Standard Silver: Coin: Sterling.*

ALM'S BASIN or DISH — For collection of alms in church.

Early examples very ornate and varied in shape: later a plain basin or plate.

AMERICAN MAKERS' MARKS. See *Dies* — Except occasionally, circa 1800, when an eagle was used by a few, no national or city marks are known, though a city name has been added to his own by several makers. The earlier silversmiths used dies of ornamental shape and sometimes a distinctive symbol: the later ones employed initials or names usually in plain oblongs or ovals. Some makers had more than one mark and even used them on the same piece. Within the last twenty years much work has been done in identifying the marks and studying the lives of the men, but many puzzles remain. A list of known American silversmiths, of whom a large number worked before 1800, and reproductions of the marks of many of them are given in this volume. The shape of the die is always to be noted. Besides the general outline of the marks, for which see *Dies,* the following are some of the devices used:

crescent	☾
crown	♔
fleur de lys	⚜
pellet	•
star	★
sun	☀

ARABESQUE — Chased decoration on a silver surface consisting of geometrical patterns, scrolls, strapwork, mingled with occasional fruits, flowers and figures.

B

BAIL — The handle of a kettle or basket, fitted to its centre

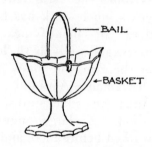

and from which the basket hangs. Of various shapes and often richly elaborate.

BALUSTER STEM — See *Stem*.

BAND — A ridge or belt, usually plain but sometimes ribbed or decorated, about the main body of a vessel. See *Tankard*.

BAPTISMAL BASIN — A large round deep platter with broad edge and usually domed in the centre. Common in XVIII Century.

BASE — The bottom or lowest member of a utensil: that upon which it stands unless there are balls or feet.

BASKET — To hold bread or cake. A shallow dish on a moulded base, swung from a bail or handle: of any shape: may be solid but often of cut work or of silver wire. Popular in England middle XVIII Century, being made of silver or of Sheffield plate following the lines of silver design.

BEADED — A form of decoration much used at end of

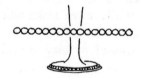

XVIII Century for rims and edges: a row of tiny balls adjoining, like a string of beads.

BEAKER — A cylindrical drinking vessel with slightly

flared lip and flat bottom or moulded base with or without handles.

Those tall in proportion to their diameter or with two handles were usually sacramental pieces, while the short ones and those with one handle were ordinarily in domestic service.

BEVELLED — Sloping: members of an article, e.g., mouldings, arranged at an angle.

BEZEL —The projecting flange or lip inside a cover or lid fitting the latter to the body of the vessel proper. See *illustration of Coffee Pot.*

BLACK-JACK—A drinking ves-

sel made of leather with

tapering or barrel-shaped body and silver rim, sometimes with silver base, band and handle.

Made in England and Teutonic countries before 1600 but not in America. See *Bombard.*

BODY — The main part of a silver vessel. In a tankard the part which contains the liquid, etc.

BODY DROP — A ridge on the body of a tankard under the upper end of the handle, sometimes slightly decorated, usually found on the earlier pieces. See *Rat Tail* and *Tankard.*

BOMBARD — A leathern flagon with silver trimmings used in England before 1600. See *Black-jack.*

BONBONNIERE — A small dish of any shape for holding bonbons on the table. Modern.

BOSS — A protuberant ornament.

BOWL — A receptacle, round or oval, deep in proportion to diameter and of some size, standing on splayed base or rim and with rounded bottom inside.

BRAZIER — A stand on feet, usually with wooden handle, to hold hot coals — later a

spirit lamp to heat a dish placed upon it. Forerunner of the chafing dish.

BRIGHT CUT — Incised decoration on a silver surface — e.g., a spoon handle — forming a pattern. Used 1780 et seq.

BULBOUS — In bulb form. Used sometimes in describing the body of a vessel.

BUTTER TESTER — A hollow silver tube slightly conical in form with cutting edge at smaller end and ring or handle at other end used for plunging into butter for testing the quality of its mass.

C

CABRIOLE LEGS — Bandy legs:

goatlike.

CADDY — A receptacle for holding tea leaves.

CADDY SPOON — A short handled scoop for taking tea out of the caddy.

CAN (*formerly* Cann) — A drinking vessel with curved body, single or double scroll handle, rounded bottom and

splayed base without a cover.

CANDELABRUM — A candlestick with central stem and two or more branches fitted with sockets.

CANDLESTICK — A utensil with base, stem and socket or pin to hold a candle erect, of varying shape and ornamentation: such as a fluted or reeded column with capital of one of the orders: a baluster stem with irregular base and socket: festooned with flowers, medallions and other devices: socket sometimes removable.

CARTOUCHE — A symmetrical ornamental tablet used in the decoration of or the engraving on a silver vessel. A conventional figure usually symmetrical enclosing makers' marks as:

CASTERS — Small bottles of glass or vessels of silver, with pierced detachable tops

for sprinkling food with pepper, salt, sugar, etc. See *Muffineer*. May be round or octagonal, plain or decorated.

CAUDLE CUP — A squat drinking vessel with moulded base, bellied sides

and two handles: so called from "caudle," a warm spiced drink of ale or wine. Primarily in domestic use but later in sacramental service.

CHALICE — A conventional sacramental cup on a baluster stem with flat base.

In use from an early period. Often richly decorated and worked.

CHASED — Decorated by chiselling, as a silver surface.

CHOCOLATE POT — Like a cof-

fee pot, except that the

thicker contents require an open instead of a pipe spout.

CIBORIUM — A covered vessel to contain the "host" in church. May be in chalice form with domed cover.

CISTERN — A huge bowl for cooling bottles of wine.

COASTER — A small bottle stand for table, used to save the cloth from drippings:

usually round, with a wooden bottom, and silver side an inch or so in height. Occasionally on wheels.

COFFEE POT—XVIII Century and since. A tall receptacle for holding and serving coffee after it is made. The

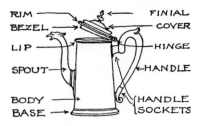

essentials are the body, the spout, the lid, the handle, the base. The normal type has a round pot larger at the bottom, a trumpet base,

a curved spout, cover with finial and scrolled wooden handle. Many variations, however, are found.

COFFEE SPOON — A small spoon for after-dinner coffee with shorter handle than the tea spoon. Not earlier than XVIII Century.

COIN — This word stamped by a die on silver after 1837 designated that the metal was of the same fineness as silver money, then and now .900 fine, i.e., 10% alloy. This fineness is also sometimes indicated by the letters C (coin) or D (dollar) stamped on silver. See *Sterling*.

COVER — See *Lid*.

CREAMER — A small vessel to hold cream for tea and

therefore not antedating 1700. The earlier type is

plain, round, with splayed base and double scroll handle. Repoussé ornament was sometimes used. Then came the tiny round pitcher with a long spout and three cabriole legs. By 1790 the helmet shape came in fashion with a square base, and later still the oval jug on its own bottom. In the elaborate tea set of 1810 and later the cream pitcher became much larger and matched teapot and sugar bowl in decoration.

CRUET-STAND — A frame consisting of flat base on feet with an upper level pierced and handle above, to hold cruets or casters for pepper, oil, vinegar, etc.

CUP — The generic name for

a drinking vessel without cover unless specified. Usually a vessel of beaker form but with rounded lower body, plain, fluted or gadrooned, and a flat, or splayed base.

CUSPED — A form in which two curves meet in a point

as frequently used in the shape of a purchase of a tankard lid.

CUT CARD ORNAMENT — A pattern — leaves for example — cut from sheet metal and applied to the sides and covers of dishes.

CUT SILVER — A plain surface ornamented by pierced work i.e., having a pattern stamped out. Useful only for solids. Much used in the bread and cake baskets of middle XVIII Century, and for borders as of coasters.

D

DESSERT SPOON — Between a table and tea spoon in size. XIX Century.

DIES —The metal object cut to impress devices, such as makers' marks on silver by pressure or by blow. The

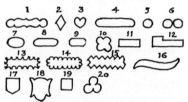

1-CARTOUCHE. 2-DIAMOND. 3-HEART. 4-LONG OVAL. 5-CIRCLE. 6-DOUBLE CIRCLE. 7-OVAL. 8-OVAL, FLAT. 9-OCTAGON. 10-QUATRE FOIL. 11-RECTANGLE. 12-R., SHAPED. 13-R., ENGRAILED. 14-R., SCALLOPED. 15-R., SERRATED. 16-SCROLL. 17-SHIELD. 18-SHAPED SHIELD. 19-SQUARE. 20-TREFOIL.

shapes when used for marks are important and among them the ones above are noted.

DISH — A deep vessel to hold food, with rim and (usually) cover, between a plate and a bowl. Two handles if any in same plane as the rim.

DISH CROSS — A skeleton of pivoted crossed arms with lamp or place for same in

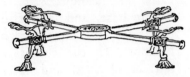

centre to heat a dish set upon sliding rests provided with feet supporting the cross.

DISH RING — See *Potato Ring*.

DRAM CUP — A small shallow circular cup from two to three inches in diameter with one or two ear-shaped

handles on side, used for taking a dram of medicine. Erroneously called winetasters of late.

DROP — The slightly moulded point of union between the handle and the back of bowl in a spoon. Sometimes double. See *Body Drop*.

E

ECUELLA — A shallow bowl, round or oval, with two handles, for broth. The handles are often longitudinal as in the American porringer. Body of dish may be richly decorated and fluted, cover as well.

EMBOSSED — Decorated with figures or ornament in relief made by a die or tool upon a smooth surface.

ENGRAILED — A border composed of a series of semicircular indents. The reverse of scalloped. See *Dies*.

EPERGNE — An elaborate centre piece for table decoration. The later designs included slender standards on a richly worked base with branches holding baskets and even sockets for candles, or perhaps a solid centre holding a fruit basket with smaller baskets around this superstructure.

ESCUTCHEON — An heraldic term used in silver to describe the ornamented place, often shield-shaped, where the owner's arms or initials are engraved. A plate surrounding a keyhole.

EWER — A large pitcher, varying in shape, holding water for rinsing the hands at meals. In use before forks; being handed about with a basin.

F

— A stamp occasionally placed upon foreign plate imported into England to indicate its assay and sterling quality. A modern usage.

FEET — In place of a solid base an object will often be

supported by three or four legs and the feet in which they terminate.

Ball and Claw. A foot composed of a ball grasped by an animal's or bird's claw.

Ball. A foot in oval or round form.

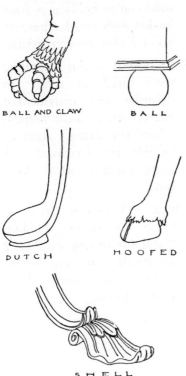

BALL AND CLAW   BALL

DUTCH   HOOFED

SHELL

Dutch. A foot in form of a disc standing flat or raised slightly on a shoe. The usual leg being bandied.

Hoofed. A foot carved to resemble a hoof.

Shell. A terminal of a leg in ribbed shell form.

FINE SILVER — Pure silver.

FINIAL — The decorative apex of an object. A small cast ornament to finish the lid or cap of an article; frequently used in tankards, casters, pots, etc. See *Tankard.*

FLAGON — An elongated tankard of large size used as a pitcher, sometimes provided

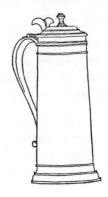

with a lip or spout. Found frequently in the Communion sets. The later forms are ewer-shaped.

FLASK — A receptacle for liquids shaped like an animal or bird, or of conventional form, flattened and rounded.

FLAT WARE — The trade name for knives, forks and spoons.

FLEUR DE LYS — A conven-

tional lily shape often used with silversmith's marks.

FLIP STRAW — A small hollow tube of silver used instead of a straw for drinking flip or other hot or frothy drinks.

FLUTED — A surface ornamented by parallel channels or grooves usually running up and down, like the fluted stem of a candlestick.

FOLIATED — Ornamented with conventionalized representation of leaves and branches.

FORK — Until XVIII Century of steel with ivory, porcelain or other handles. Silver forks of two tines were, however, known in Italy prior to this, and the first in England had

but two. Forks of three, and later of four prongs, followed. By 1760–70, four tines were common in France and England, but not freely made in America until circa 1800. The fork handle followed the type and design of the spoon handle.

FROSTED WORK — A silver surface finely roughened.

FUNNEL — An article of the shape of an inverted hollow cone or hemisphere terminating below in a straight or curved pipe used

in decanting wine and liquors. It was usually fitted with a strainer and occasionally attached to a small tray. The wine funnel of silver or glass was considered essential when wine or spirits were served outside the original bottle.

G

GADROONED OR GODROONED (*latter modern spelling*) — A surface ornamented by a series of curved convex ruffles or ridges called gadroons va-

rying in form but joined at their extremities, being in a measure the reverse of fluted. Though long in use it was a favorite decoration in the teapots of 1810–1830. In abbreviated form, the rim of a vessel as well as parts of a base are often similarly treated.

GOBLET — A chalice-shaped drinking cup. See *Chalice.*

GRACE CUP — See *Mazer.*

GRAVY SPOON — A very large spoon of the shape and type of a table spoon. Common in England in XVIII Century, but few made in America.

H

HALL MARKS — Ten cities in Great Britain were authorized to assay and stamp plate through their "halls" or Goldsmith Companies. For full details consult the works of Jackson or Cripps. London may illustrate the system of marks. Nationality is indicated by a lion passant (regardant until 1822). The city mark is a leopard's head varying in details. Alphabets of twenty letters, Roman capitals and script and Black letter capitals and script alternating irregularly, indicate the year. The maker has his mark and in 1784, a sovereign's head was added as a fifth stamp. Each mark is also helped in its significance for its cycle by the shape of its die. A certain usage prevails as to where the marks are set on different articles, e.g., in spoons on the back of the handle well down. English silver can be more accurately dated by this system than any other nationality. *Pseudo Hall marks.* — In America after 1800 marks resembling English hall marks were often placed on silver, such as a letter, a line, a head or sheaf of wheat, a bee hive, etc. These are easily distinguished from true hall marks and should not be confused with them. They occasionally had some significance as in Baltimore.

HANAP — See *Standing Cup and Cover.*

HANDLE — That part of an

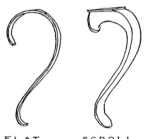

FLAT   SCROLL

article by which it is grasped. See *Bail.*

1. *Flat Handle.* A thin flat band, sometimes corrugated, in scroll shape.

2. *Scroll Handle.* Like a letter S with lower half shrunk.

3. *Double Scroll Handle.* A handle formed of two scrolls.

DOUBLE SCROLL   KEY HOLE

4. *Strap Handle.* See *Flat Handle.*

5. *Pierced Handle.* A pierced silver plate as with porringer.

6. *Keyhole.* Used to indicate the ordinary form of porringer handle in which one of the openings resembles a keyhole.

7. *Geometrical.* A porringer handle, the openings in and

GEOMETRIC   WOODEN

the exterior form of which

is made in geometrical patterns.

8. *Urn and Crown.* A porringer handle in which the
piercings are so shaped as
to form a crowned urn.

9. *Wooden Handle.* A
straight turned or a curved
wooden grip fitting into and

pinned through silver
sockets.

HINGE — The device of over-
lapping edges, pierced and
held by a pin, which fastens
a lid to an article while
permitting it to swing.

HOLLOW WARE — The trade
name for all sorts of dishes
vessels, cups, bowls, etc.

I

INCISED — Engraved, cut or
stamped in. Used occasionally in describing certain
silversmith's marks in con-
tradistinction to the result
produced by the usual em-
bossing die.

INDENTED — Notched, as in
a border, with teeth or
indents.

INTERLACED — Lines which
weave under and over each
other as in engraved decoration.

J

JUG — A deep plain vessel for
holding and pouring liquids
with handle, flat base, circular body and possibly a

small nose. A pitcher, usually of earthenware, mounted
in silver.

K

KETTLE — A silver vessel with spout and bail on a stand with lamp to heat water

for tea. English tea kettles of second half XVIII Century are often of great beauty in shape and decoration. The bail may be wound with rattan or insulated. No definite type.

KNIVES — Table utensils consisting of cutting blades, usually of steel, later of silver, fastened to handles of silver.

KNOP — The bulge or knob midway in the stem of a chalice, for convenience in holding.

L

LABEL — The inscribed metal ticket hung by a chain about a decanter, to indicate its contents.

LACQUERED — Covered with a thin coating of transparent shellac to prevent silver from tarnishing.

LADLE — A round or oval bowl with a handle set usually at an angle to the plane of the bowl.

A soup ladle is large with a handle sharply curved, less often straight.

A punch ladle is small with straight twisted whalebone handle fitting in a socket.

A cream or gravy ladle is like a small soup ladle.

LEGS — Owing to their insignificance legs are seldom referred to in describing silver, the words foot or feet being preferred. Technically, however, that part of the support between the body and the foot proper, as in the case of Dutch, hoofed or shell and sometimes claw feet is the leg. This frequently is bandied in form.

LID — The cover of a vessel, usually hinged. See *Tankard*.

LIP — The edge of a drinking vessel to which the mouth is applied.

LOVING CUP — A modern untechnical term to denote a large cup on a high base with two or three handles and without lid or cover.

LOZENGE — Diamond shaped.

M

MACE — A club-shaped staff or wand of office borne before mayor's, bailiffs, or other officers by their sergeants. Silver maces were only occasionally used in America.

MARKS STAMPED ON SILVER — These must always be distinguished from owners' or other marks, engraved upon silver articles.

Die marks were intended to indicate the silversmith, the place of origin, often the date of making, sometimes the nationality also. A considerable number of pieces in all countries seem never to have been marked. A hall or Government stamp guaranteed the fineness of the alloy after testing.

For British marks, see *Hall Marks;* for American Makers' Marks, see that title.

European silver is usually stamped with a city mark and the chiffre or initials of the maker. Some of these city marks give the exact or approximate date. Thus according to Rosenberg the number of dots in the Augsburg pine cone has a date significance; Liège and Copenhagen used actual numerals; Paris had a series of alphabets crowned, the date letter thus giving the year.

The makers' marks or initials in a die of special shape have been largely gathered in Rosenberg "Der Goldschmiede Merkzeichen," Frankfurt, 2nd ed., which consult.

MARROW SPOON — A spoon with narrow, elongated

blunt bowl, and still narrower grooved handle, thus forming a union of two scoops of differing widths for the extraction of marrow from a bone.

MASK — A grotesque head or face often used at the lower end or tip of a tankard handle.

MAZER — An antique drinking bowl shaped like a section of a sphere, banded and mounted in silver, though ordinarily of wood. Rarely on a splayed foot and with a cover, in squat chalice form. Sometimes called a Grace Cup.

MEASURE — An open drinking vessel of standard sizes used for measuring liquids. Usually mug or can shape and frequently stamped with the capacity held.

MEDALLION — A round or oval disk decorated with heads or figures; usually cast like a coin, but sometimes inset in a dish or tankard.

MID BAND — See *Band.*

MONSTRANCE — Once a reliquary. Since XIV Century the public receptacle for showing the consecrated host; of glass and precious metal with stones often inlaid; varied in form; sometimes like a candelabrum spired.

MONTEITH — A large punch bowl whose rim — usually

movable — is notched and is said to hold wine glasses by the foot, though few examples have ever been found where drinking vessels could be so supported. XVIII Century.

MOTE SPOON—A spoon with pierced bowl. Small ones with pointed handles were used for tea, while larger with long handles were used for wine and the communion. See *tea spoon*.

MOULDING — An ornamentation made by grooved or raised bands usually applied to the base, rim or edge of silver articles, but occasionally elsewhere, as in the mid band.

MOUNT — A general term to include the metal base, moulding, rim, cover clamp, or other accessory by which a utensil of wood, pottery, porcelain, or other material is decorated and adapted for use. Also the ornamental accessories of sword hilt and scabbard.

MUFFINEER — An upright article of table furniture usually round, with moulded

base and pierced detachable cap, for sprinkling sugar. A sugar caster, XVIII Century.

MUG — A drinking vessel with straight or tapering sides, scroll handle with flat bot-

tom, moulded base and no lid. In the earthenware mugs of European make a silver lid is sometimes clamped to the handle.

N

NAUTILUS CUP — A nautilus shell mounted as a drinking vessel in metal with stem and base, a European fashion XVI and XVII Centuries.

NEF — A cup in the shape of a ship.

NULLED — Ornamented with a convex rounded decoration differing from a gadroon in that the latter is on a rounded, while the former is on a flat or quarter round surface.

NUTMEG GRATER — A utensil containing a roughened surface for grating nutmegs. Frequently ingeniously designed with a receptacle for holding the nutmeg when not in use and often made pocket size.

P

PANELLED — Decorated with small surfaces framed either by mouldings, engraving or by the outline of the piece itself.

PAP BOAT — A small open boat-shaped vessel without feet or cover, but with lip

designed for use in feeding infants and invalids.

PAP SPOON — A spoon with bowl partly covered, for feeding infants and invalids.

PARCEL GILT — Silver or other metal partially gilded as a band around the rim of a beaker, an escutcheon, the interior of a cup, or a more elaborate decoration where portions of the chased or repousse work are done in gold.

PATCH BOX — A small carved box of varying form and

decoration used for carrying court plaster patches.

PATEN — A round plate or flat dish to hold the sacramental bread at communion service, in connection with

the chalice. For wafers only it was sometimes fitted to the chalice as a cover. Used occasionally for domestic service on the table as a salver.

PATINA — The finish of a surface obtained by age and use.

PEG — One of a set of pins fixed at intervals in a drinking vessel to measure the quantity which each drinker was to take.

PELLET — A small rounded boss used as a period or decoration in makers' marks, as ●

Box PEPPER — Small, round

or many-sided vessels, with

flat bottom, moulded, and with removable pierced cover and handle, used for sprinkling food with pepper.

PEPPER CASTER — See *Caster.*

PIE OR CAKE LIFTER — An article shaped like a mason's trowel, usually pierced. Made in England as early as 1765.

PILGRIM BOTTLE — A flask-shaped bottle with chains and a stopper. English XVII Century.

PIN — The small, cylindrical piece of silver, used to hold two parts of a hinge together.

PLATE — Generic term for silver utensils in the mass. In XVI Century silver bullion. A flat, shallow dish with edge, round, oval or octagonal, for holding food.

PLATTER — A large plate for serving food, usually oval or octagonal.

PLAQUE — A plate, or flat panel, of thin silver, generally ornamented in repoussé.

PORRINGER — 1. *English Type.* A two-handled cup,

with flat or moulded base, straight sides and a cover; XVII and XVIII Centuries,

ENGLISH

AMERICAN

often gadrooned or repoussé. See *Caudle Cup* and *Posset Cup*.

2. *American Type.* A round, shallow saucepan, with flat base and a flat triangular handle nearly flush with the rim, of pierced work. The earlier design was geometrical, changing about 1735–1745 into the keyhole shape so-called from the final aperture.

PORRINGER SPOON — A spoon slightly smaller than the modern desert spoon, used with a porringer.

POSNET — A small pot with handle and three feet used for boiling (English).

POSSET CUP — See *Caudle Cup*. Posset was milk curdled with wine with spices added. Hot ale also sometimes used.

POT — A large round receptacle for hot liquids, e. g., a hot water pot for ceremonial tea. Japanese.

POTATO RING — A large open work splayed circlet without cover or base, circa 4 in. in

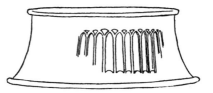

height, Irish, XVIII Century. Potatoes were heaped on a napkin inside of ring.

POUNCED — Ornamented by a series of minute indentations made by a fine punch. Often used as a relief to more elaborate decoration.

PRICKET — The spike at the top of a candlestick upon which the candle was thrust. Still used in church candelabra.

PSEUDO HALL MARKS — See *Hall Marks*.

[153]

PURCHASE — The thumbpiece of a tankard; the lid is raised by the drinker's thumb acting upon a protuberance next the handle.

This may be a simple knob, ribbed upright, or double spiral; or it may be a lion, water witch, eagle, or other object in great variety.

Q

QUATREFOIL — An ornamental figure having four cuspid divisions, usually formed by segments of a circle. See *Dies*.

R

RAILING — An open fret raised from the surface as used in trays, coasters, etc. Sometimes called gallery.

RAT TAIL — The ridge extension of the handle under the bowl of a spoon, first half XVIII Century. Rarely

used also as part of the decoration of a tankard

body under the handle. See *Drop* and *Body Drop*.

REEDED — A surface ornamented by a series of paral-

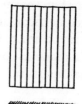

lel ridges running up and down. The opposite of fluted.

REPOUSSÉ — A raised pattern or ornament made by beating a thin metal from the

reverse side with hammer and punches.

RIM — In general the upper edge of any dish or vessel or the lower edge of a cover. The rim of a drinking vessel is, however, preferably referred to as the lip.

ROCOCO — Florid ornamentation consisting of scroll, shells, etc., thrown together without proper connection.

ROSE — A design in the form of a conventionalized single

rose, found occasionally in makers' marks. See *John Hull's Mark*.

ROSE WATER DISH — A large richly ornamented basin for rinsing the fingers at table.

S

SALTS — Receptacles for salt, articles of table furniture, in mediaeval times, of great distinction. As made by

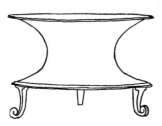

colonial silversmiths, salt cellars were mainly (*a*) built up in a series of mouldings from a larger base with a splayed top in which a depression held the salt, or (*b*) a small round or oval

dish on three or four legs. See *Trencher Salts*.

Abroad, massive cellars or standing salts, similar to cut, were used early; while in later times small silver vessels frequently pierced, containing glass salt holders, were in vogue for individual use.

SALVER — In its early form the salver, often richly decorated, was used with the ewer for rinsing the fingers. After forks became customary, the salver as a tray with a low moulded scalloped or gadrooned edge, was used for dishes, plates, cards, and many other purposes. Decoration generally of chased work.

SAUCE BOAT — A boat-shaped dish, generally on short legs, with spout and high curved handle at end, for sauces and

gravies, XVIII Century. The earliest had spout at each end and handles at the side.

SCALLOPED — A border composed of a series of semi-circular or otherwise curved projections, the reverse of engrailed. See *Dies*.

SCENT JAR — A vessel, shaped like a porcelain jar, with detached cover; often repoussé; to hold lavender, rose leaves, and the like.

SCONCE — A wall bracket to hold candles. The essential parts are the wall plate and socket; the arm, usually scrolled, fitting into said

socket; and third the candle holder and bobeche to catch

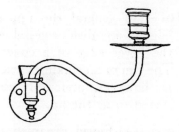

drippings. There is no one recognized type.

SCROLLED — Surface decorated with scroll work either chased or repoussé.

SERRATED — A border composed of saw-toothed notches. See *Dies*.

SHOE — A thin plate on the bottom of a foot.

SIPHON — A silver tube gracefully bent and often in-

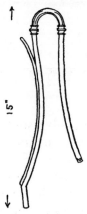

geniously contrived for siphoning liquids, as wine or spirits, from cask or bottle to decanter.

SKEWER — A solid pointed flat tongue of silver, with a ring in or on the broad end. To pin a round of beef or other articles of food together for the oven and to be withdrawn when carved.

SNUFF BOX — A pocket receptacle for snuff, with hinged lid, often richly chased or worked.

SNUFFERS AND TRAY — A scissors-like contrivance for snuffing a candle and catching the wick end. Usually fitted with a tray. The oldest, noted, by an American maker, is 1750.

SOCKET — The hollow into which something is fitted, as the handle of a teapot into the body; the arm of a sconce into the plate; a candle into the candlestick.

SOFFIT — The under horizontal surface of a moulding.

SPLAYED BASE — The outturned flaring but squat

base moulding and neck,

supporting an object such as a can, coffee pot, etc.

SPOON —A handle and bowl solidly joined in the same plane to carry liquid to the mouth in small quantities.

1. *Round bowl,* or slightly pear shaped with various handles, in a few cases bowl and handle soldered together; in many cases a crystal bowl fastened to a metal handle. This type lasted until circa 1700.

2. *Oval Bowl.* Throughout XVIII Century. The oval bowl which came in near its beginning has tended to become less and less a perfect oval and more ovoid, so that generally speaking the sharper the point of the spoon, the later its date.

3. *Egg Shaped Bowl.* The perfect oval is rarely seen after 1750, being replaced by the egg shape which has persisted ever since.

4. *Round and Octagonal Handle.* This was usual with the earlier spoons, being often twisted, or in Norway and Sweden flat and twisted, or flat enlarged at the end and chased.

5. *Flat Handle.* With the

oval bowl came in the flat solid handle united to the bowl by a ridge of union

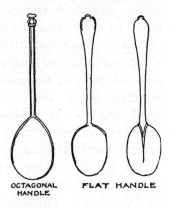

OCTAGONAL HANDLE   FLAT HANDLE

beneath (rat tail) which was ribbed and later plain. The handle end was first broadened, notched twice (trifid) and turned up slightly; later broadened, rounded with a blunt point and turned back. The latest type of handle associated with the oval bowl had a rounded end ridged above.

6. *Sloped or Shaped Handles*. This name is given to describe the next type of handle with a rounded or pointed end sloping to its junction with the bowl which often appeared as a drop (q.v.), a partial survival of the rat tail. By 1770–80, such handles be-

gan to be chased with bright cut ornament or feather

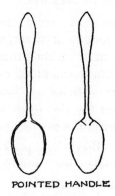

POINTED HANDLE

edging and an escutcheon. (q.v.)

7 *Coffin Handle*. For a decade circa 1800, the rounded

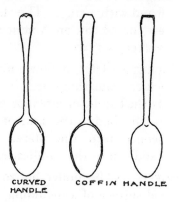

CURVED HANDLE   COFFIN HANDLE

handle ended in an elongated octagon like the head of a coffin.

8. *Fiddle Back Handle*. But by 1810 this changed to a flat handle, broad half way

to the bowl and then shaped

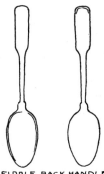

FIDDLE BACK HANDLE

in. Subsequently all types were followed.

SPOUT — The tube, trough or opening through which the contents of pot, pan, flagon, pitcher, etc. are poured. Varying from the curved or long straight pipe of a teapot, or coffee pot, to the mere bend in the rim of a saucepan.

SPOUT CUP — A small plain covered cup with a curved

tube like spout. For an invalid's use in bed.

STANDARD SILVER — This term represents fixed proportions of pure silver combined with alloy as directed by law. The standards have varied from time to time. See *Sterling and Coin.*

STANDING CUP AND COVER — A cup of some size and splendour to serve the master's wine. So notable sometimes as to have a special name. The bowl might be an ostrich egg, or cocoanut or even of wood as well as of silver or crystal. Tall usually with a stem and richly decorated. Frequent in Germany with a human figure standing on the cover.

STEEPLE CUP — A standing cup, q.v., with steeple surmounting the cover.

STEM — The member of a vase, chalice, candlestick, or cup which unites receptacle and base.
Baluster Stem. Bulging like a baluster.

STERLING — About 1857 the word Sterling was stamped on silver articles to indicate its fineness, as .925, meaning 925 parts pure silver with 75 parts by weight of pure copper in every 1000 parts. This is the same as the English standard of allowing but 18 dwt of alloy and 11 ounces, 2 dwt silver in each 12 ounces. See *Coin*.

STRAINER — A circular shallow bowl of small diameter perforated with holes, usually in a symmetrical pat-

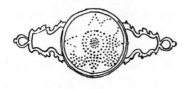

tern. For a tea cup a single clip or handle is used. The teapot spout strainer is a modern idea. For a punch bowl the strainer was fitted with two skeleton handles in the same plane and thus stretched from rim to rim. Handles often gracefully curved.

STRAP WORK — A form of decoration simulating interlaced bands, made by chasing on silver, or less often by interwoven metal strips.

SUGAR BOWL — Receptacle for sugar in use on the table, always with a cover. The early type was round on a splayed base, somewhat pear shaped with a lid and finial. The urn type, slim with square base and domed or even pointed cover, succeeded to be followed by an oval shape on a high base with two high shouldered strap handles. Then came the tea set period.

SUGAR SIFTER — A ladle-shaped spoon, the round bowl of which is pierced for sprinkling sugar upon food.

SUGAR TONGS — A tweezer-like article for grasping a lump of sugar. Commonly two arms of solid or pierced work ending in spoon or other tips and broad at their junction. Exceedingly common 1800–1825 and since. An early variant is in the form of scissors of ingenious decorated designs, often with cutting edges for breaking the lumps.

SUN — A conventional emblem used in some makers' marks. See *Robt. Sanderson's mark*.

T

TANKARD — A drinking vessel on a flat or moulded base or low foot, with tapering or bellied sides, handle and

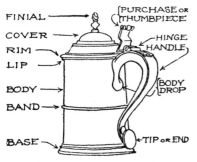

FINIAL ⟶ PURCHASE OR THUMBPIECE
COVER ⟶
RIM ⟶ HINGE
LIP ⟶ HANDLE
BODY ⟶ BODY DROP
BAND ⟶
BASE ⟶ TIP OR END

lid. Known in flagon form in England about 1550, but not in common use until a century later. The early American tankards had a flat lid to which later a low dome was added. Later still the lid consisted of a series of steps usually surmounted by a finial. To describe these three species of lid (the lid more than any other feature distinguishes a tankard), the terms flat, domed, stepped, and stepped and domed, are used. A band was added to the body about 1710 and

usually accompanies the domed lid.

TAZZA — A drinking cup consisting of a shallow bowl like that of a champagne glass, on a baluster stem and splayed base like a chalice. XVI Century.

TEA CADDY — A covered receptacle for tea to be used on the tea table, varying in shape from rectangular to round, from a box to a vase, sometimes fitted with lock and key. XVIII Century.

TEAPOT — A pot for the making and distribution of tea, with lid, spout and handle. A few instances prior to 1725; common after 1750. An early type was *globular* on a moulded base with semicircular handle and short spout. Then succeeded the bell shape with long curved spout and perhaps a double scroll handle. The pear-shaped teapot was the next fashion, often richly chased or repoussé to be followed by an oval or octagonal form often on its own stand, and with a straight

GLOBULAR

BELL SHAPED

PEAR SHAPED

OVAL

spout. After perhaps 1800–1810 the elaborate tea set of three or four pieces was customary where the teapot was large, with heavy ornament and a much curved spout. In all the various shapes there are knobs or

finials for the lids, and sockets for the wooden handles. Since about 1815 the shape, size and ornamentation of the teapot have varied endlessly.

TEA SPOON — A spoon of small size, adapted to a tea cup. For types see *Spoon*. A spoon with pierced bowl and round, sharp, pointed handle, was used in XVIII Century to remove tea leaves and free the teapot spout. See *Mote Spoon*.

TEA URN — A hot water heater in urn shape with square base on feet, a faucet, two curved handles and a high domed cover with finial. Second half XVIII Century. The contents were in earliest form heated by a cylindrical piece of iron or hot charcoal dropped into a container from the top. Later a burner, finally a lamp, were placed below the urn.

THUMBPIECE. See *Purchase*.

TINDER BOX — A small silver box, usually of pocket size, made with a piece of steel on the outside in position to be struck by a flint, which together with the tinder is kept inside the box when not in use.

TINE — The prong with which a fork is armed for piercing food.

TODDY — A mixture of spirits and hot water sweetened.

TODDY CUP — Spoon and strainer. Small silver utensils used in making toddy.

TOUCHSTONE — A fine, smooth black stone, used for testing the fineness of silver, by comparing the color of the streak made by rubbing on the metal with that made by silver of a known standard, called the touch needle.

TRAY — See *Salver*. A shallow, flat-bottomed receptacle, with or without feet, varying in shape and size, with straight, curved or sloped edges. Used like salver. Occasionally shaped to fit a teapot or other object.

TRENCHER SALTS — Small, solid salt cellars, circular, oval, octagonal or triangu-

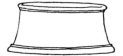

lar, with the upper surface hollowed. XVII Century. See *Salts*.

TRIFID HANDLE — See *Spoon*.

TRUMPET BASE — The outturned flaring base moulding with elongated neck

supporting an object. It resembles the big end of a trumpet inverted. An American term (?).

TUMBLER — A small, round-bottomed wine cup, like a bowl without handles, common in Germany and Northern Europe in XVIII Century.

W

WAITER — An untechnical term for a large tray, usually without feet, to carry plate or a tea or coffee service. Handles are customary.

WINE-TASTER — A small, shallow, solid saucer with one or two handles, for testing the flavor and odor of wine. French. Much like the dram cup.

WHISTLE; WHISTLING TANK-ARD — The lower end of a scrolled hollow tankard, handle was usually provided with an opening used as a vent during soldering. Very rarely, if ever, have vent and tip been used to form the whistle popularly but erroneously supposed to have been for calling the tap drawer. Whistling tankard is, therefore, a misnomer.